BEYOND ADDICTION

Sally Discovers How to Think for Herself

Alexander T. Polgar, Ph. D.

Sandriam Publications Inc.
Hamilton, Ontario, Canada

Beyond Addiction: Sally Discovers How to Think for Herself
©2020 Sandriam Publications Inc.

183 St Clair Blvd.
Hamilton, Ontario, Canada
L8M 2N9
atpolgar@sympatico.ca
www.atpolgar.com/sandriampublications

All rights reserved
No part of this book may be reproduced, stored in a retrieval system or transmitted in any form or by any means, electronic, mechanical, microfilming, recording, or otherwise, without written permission from the publisher.

ISBN: 978-1-7771669-3-9

Printed and bound in Canada

Cover: Workhorse Design Studio

ALSO, BY ALEXANDER T. POLGAR, PH.D.

Conducting Parenting Capacity Assessments: A Manual for Mental Health Professionals

Chronobiology: Strategies for Coping With Shift Work

Because We Can – We Must: Achieving the Human Developmental Potential in Five Generations

TWO: One Destined to Addiction the Other to be Free

Freedom: Sally Gets Sober and Starts to Grow Up

Finding Purpose and Meaning: Sally Survives Her Brief, Nasty Dance With Psychiatry

Dedicated to all past and present victims of tribal oppression, hatred, and violence.

CONTENTS

Breaking the Tribal Chains 1
Chapter 1 Tribalism 5
Chapter 2 The Myth of Hard-Wired Tribalism 11
Chapter 3 Instead of Progress, We Settle for Change 17
Chapter 4 The Prodigal Son 23
Chapter 5 Nihil Sub Sole Novum: Nothing New Under the Sun 29
Chapter 6 The Benefits and Cost of Tribalism 37
Chapter 7 Reality Instead of Platitudes 47
Chapter 8 What Will it Take? 53
Chapter 9 Being Social Without Being Tribal 61
Reflections 69
    Introduction 70
    A Working Hypothesis 73
    Competition 76
    The Indigenous Canadian Experience 78
    Structure and Content 84
    History of Drug and Alcohol Use 87
    Insidious Biology 90
    It's All About Prevention 92
    On Being a Developmentalist 94
    What is Your Conceptual Framework? 96
References 101
Other references to tribalism 107
Acknowledgements 109
About the Author 111

BREAKING THE TRIBAL CHAINS

I am Sally, and this last book completes the trilogy about my journey from life as an addicted addict to abstinence from all intoxicating legal and illegal drugs. Of course, when I started, the trilogy was meant to be three very readable books, which I hoped would help people like me and those who care about us. That was until I noticed this stone in my shoe. At first, I ignored it, expecting to get used to it, but that did not happen. The stone became increasingly bothersome until I could no longer stand it and had to do something about it.

You guessed it: the stone in my shoe was my constant butting heads with various tribes during my life-journey. While not a pleasant experience, I was at first able to shrug it off. This became increasingly difficult. The more I thought about these experiences, the more I got to understanding what was going on, and the more upset I became. Then my curiosity kicked in and, as is now my very familiar habit, I started reading anything I could get my eyes on about tribes. I quickly learned tribes have been around forever, and they do very bad things to their members and to other tribes. Worst of all, I came to the realization that I had been, and was still, in a tribe. This way of being did not sit well with me, and I set out to drastically change it.

This book therefore, is all about tribalism although you would not know it from the title. The word "tribal," and how being in a tribe holds us back, is not included in the title. I was told that people would not understand the idea and, as a result, would have no interest in reading this book. Since my interest is to make everyone aware of this topic, I compromised. I made the title more appealing by focusing on the benefits of growing beyond being tribal. The greatest benefit to me, as it will be to you, is discovering how to think for myself.

The trilogy then became four books. In this last book, I describe my gradual awakening and how I broke the chains that were holding me prisoner, keeping me stuck at being tribal.

Most people, including smart people whose books I read, seem not to be aware of just how problematic tribalism is to us as humans. The first chapter, therefore, is all about what it means to be tribal, and that it is caused by our obstructed development. It goes way beyond a "nation divided". In the second chapter, I go after those people who, mostly without realising it, play a big role in obstructing our development. They use the myth that tribalism is in our nature, that we are "hard-wired" for it, to keep us tribal with. That means that there is no hope of getting past it. Of course, their myth is nonsense. I and many others have gotten past being tribal. In the third chapter, I was all excited to write about my discovery that there is a big difference between change and progress. Because most people don't know this, they settle for change and never even know to look for progress - one of the reasons we continue to be stuck at being tribal.

The fourth chapter is my favourite one in this book. It is about the religious story of the Prodigal Son. I always liked the painting of it and have often wondered what the real message of the story is. I think you will like what I think the message is or at least find interesting. I won't spoil it for you here. You will have to read it for yourself.

The fifth chapter is an important one because I found out easily, just by looking, that there is nothing new about our problems being caused by being developmentally stuck at tribalism. Various people have talked about it for at least three thousand years. This, then, got me thinking about what we find so attractive about being tribal to have remained stuck there for so long. That is my focus in chapter six.

The destructive use of, in fact reliance on, platitudes (feel-good) but not true statements), is the theme of chapter seven. It is one of the main reasons we remain developmentally stuck. Instead of facing the reality that we mostly only have unachieved potential, we make up pleasing fantasies about how great we are. Those speaking platitudes include important, smart people who should but don't know better. In chapter eight, I wonder what it will take for us to realize, accept, and do something about most people being stuck at the tribal stage of development. I'm hopeful recent times just might be the perfect storm we need to finally accept tribalism as the problem and start doing what must be done to get unstuck. But to get unstuck, we need to know what that looks like. Since I have been unstuck for a while now, and I know people who have been for much longer, the last chapter, nine, is all about describing what it looks like. My plan is to show how being unstuck improves the quality of people's lives and to invite you to come along and taste the freedom.

Like in the previous three books, this one also ends with my alter ego, Dr. Polgar's, reflections. Please, indulge his almost preaching style when making some of his points. I believe he is desperate to get the most out of this last book, probably thinking he won't get another chance to influence how you think about the human condition and then what you do about it. Do have a look at his references, especially the philosophy book that reveals just how long some very smart people have identified tribalism as the cause of our human misery. Yet it continues, unless...

Chapter 1
TRIBALISM

Getting clean of all intoxicants, poisons, including tobacco and caffeine, did strange things to me. I became aware, like never before, of everything around me. All my senses came alive and I experienced the world not through a haze but through clear and brilliant sunlight. At first, it was really very weird, even scary, mostly because it was so new. Then slowly but surely, I started to like it, even to love it. For the first time in my life, everything became real.

As I said before, being real takes some getting used to, and there are many potholes on the road to starting to become human. That's why when I got straight, I talked about life being different rather than better. It was a question of which way of being I preferred. I chose to live real and experience the benefits that come with it. The benefits include not only seeing things I had not seen or did not want to see before but also becoming willing and able to talk about them. Talking about one or many elephants in the room, however, did not make me very popular. In fact, it got me into a lot of trouble. But the results, the joy, of experiencing reality, were and continue to be well-worth getting some people pissed at me.

Clean of all intoxicants and of course curious as ever, I started to think about why Alcoholics Anonymous makes such a big deal about addicts, people without pot-bellied stoves using alcohol as their drug of choice. In the same way, I got to thinking about Narcotics, Gamblers, and Sex Addicts Anonymous. I'm sure there are many other 12-Step Anonymous groups out there for all sorts of substance abuses and self-destructive activities, but I couldn't care less about what people put into their bodies or do to escape the horrible feelings that come with not having a pot-bellied stove. They are all addicts and that's all that matters - clearly, however, not to most of the world. Otherwise, a long time ago, there would only have been one 12-Step program: Addicts Anonymous.

As I was trying to understand why all kinds of people, including fancy, educated ones, act as if being an 'alcoholic' is a real thing, the light started to come on. The various 12-Step groups kind of look like, and act like they discriminate against each other. The 'alcoholics' look down on the drug users, and drug users look down on 'juicers' too sissy to stick a needle in their arm. Proudly, both announce in each meeting their drug of choice. Of course, they have little or no respect for gamblers, and sex addicts don't even count. Now, just to be fair, even if they don't look down on others, they sure see them as very different from themselves. Like a lightning bolt it struck me: I was in a tribe, and all the others were also in tribes.

Once I came to this conclusion, it was not hard to see that each tribe's identity, existence, was based on what drug or activity its members use to escape the horrible cold that it is to be an addict. I had not come all that far. Despite being totally clean, I was still in a tribe. I just exchanged one tribe, the user one, for another tribe, the non-user one. In some ways this is no better, because while I changed, I made no progress. This seemed horribly wrong to me.

This realization started me thinking about what other tribes are in my life and how I can tell them apart. It didn't take long to realize that I am surrounded by tribes and that the whole world is made up of tribes. In addition to the different addict tribes, there are religious, political, national, where you got your education, what club you belong to, where you exercise or play golf, the list is endless… tribes. Some tribes are relatively harmless, like the gym where you work out, while others are downright dangerous, like the white supremacists. Regardless of their clothes or what their clubhouse looks like, the Pope and the leader of the Hells Angels are each just boss of a tribe.

When I realised there are tribes everywhere, the next question was, what does it take to belong to a tribe? The answer is very simple. All you have to do is not think for yourself. Any tribe will do that for you very nicely. The tribe will tell you what to believe and what to value. You don't have to worry about how to behave or what to do – the tribe will tell you. Easy peasy. Just accept, for example, without question: "We exist to make you into a better person. Being a member will make you rich, famous, powerful or important. And most important, being a member will protect you from those other dangerous tribes". The list of promises, of course, goes on and on. In addition to buying into such beliefs to be a tribe member, you are required to have specific values or preferences. The values you hold can't be just willy-nilly anything. They have to be in sync with the tribe's beliefs. For example, if you are a white supremacist, a terrorist or a Holy Wars crusader of the past or present, recruiting new members is highly valued, as well as killing members of another tribe. The final requirement for membership, therefore, is that you do things that reflect, like a mirror, what you are required to believe and value.

A very messed-up way of living for a relatively newly abstinent, curious addict like myself. Not allowed to use my own mind to think, decide what to believe or value, or choose how to act in a situation… really?

The next obvious question was, "Why?" Why have people been living in tribes? Well, not really living, but warring, one tribe against another. The only answer that came to me, that made sense when I dared to think for myself, was fear.

Because I have been afraid from the beginning of my "shit life", this is an emotion I know all too well. Now I understand, however, that fear and danger are two sides of the same coin. When I was an infant, because my parents were often using, my fear was justified. I was always in danger, even of dying, because of neglect or abuse. Later, the real danger passed but the fear lingered as a constant negative emotion. I am guessing therefore, that most of the world's population, since the beginning of our time to now, have had experiences similar to mine. Fear caused by real danger, especially as children, and lingering fear often without danger, as a result of the shit environment in which they were raised. Sadly, just look at your daily newspaper, many continue to live through the same shit conditions as adults.

As a pre-teen, and then as a teen, I quickly learned the benefits of tribal membership. My tribe gave me an identity, 'user,' and unconditional acceptance for using. Also, there was something very safe and comforting about being in my tribe, even though we were all 'losers'. When I exchanged tribes to be with the non-users, this also made me feel accepted and safe. The safety and comfort of being in one or the other, however, came at a huge price. Eventually, seeing the price, I could not settle for the 'sanctuary' of the (Alcoholics Anonymous) AA tribe, especially since my fear was no longer danger-based.

From what I can see, I'm guessing most people are content to remain tribal for many reasons, especially fear - long after the danger is gone or is less intense, and long after their teenage years, I am particularly blown away by people who refer to themselves as being in a "God-Fearing" tribe. What a way to live! These and other fearful people act like they will be accepted, protected, 'saved' by their tribal membership. As a result, they seem all too willing to drink the Kool-Aid of tribal benefits. It seems to me most adults in this world live the lives of tribal teenagers, thinking and behaving like them. The only difference is, they don't look like them. Some adults, not most but some, may have a better vocabulary. This can be very misleading and cause you to have unrealistic expectations of them. You expect them to think and behave as adults, which they can't because they are adults only in their body. In their mind and/behaviour, they are developmentally stuck.

I have observed another peculiar tribal response, specifically to people who behave differently, not according to tribal rules. Outsiders are labelled as stupid, idiotic or crazy. I have been guilty of doing the same, until growing to understand that the labels do not apply. Tribal, badly-behaved, often racist, women-hating, prejudice-riddled people are not 'idiots'. They are developmentally stuck adults. Because by definition a tribe is made up of developmentally stuck adults, like the characters in the movie Mean Girls, tribes threaten, frighten, abuse, and at times, even kill each other. These conditions, since people started to write about them, have kept humans stuck in tribes looking at other tribes with suspicion, disgust, and most of all, fear.

Hopefully, all this does not sound too complicated or "airy-fairy." It really is not, once you know what to look for and think back to your full-on tribal days as a teenager. On the surface, some things have changed. The colour of your adult hair and the size of your belly might be different, and there might be more money in your pocket but underneath it all, most likely you are still in a tribe living by its required rules. Once I started to see this and to get it, I began to dislike being tribal as much as I had come to dislike psychiatry and its prescribed drugs. The next phase in my journey, the topic of this last book, therefore, is to understand this tribe-thing so I could escape from it.

I am ending this chapter with a formula that worked very well for me: I identified a serious cause of my problems, specifically my thinking and behaving as a tribal, pain-in-the-ass teenager living in an adult body. Recognising and accepting this allowed me to progress, to climb the ladder of development to heights way past the horrible tribal stage where I had been stuck. If it worked for me, it can also work for you... all of you.

Chapter 2

THE MYTH OF HARD-WIRED TRIBALISM

I am driven like a mad person to rid the world of this incredibly harmful idea that we are hard-wired to be tribal. It is a harmful idea because the message is that we cannot ever change. Since we have been tribal forever, this is taken as evidence proving the 'hard-wired' idea is true. Exceptions are treated as exceptions and the history of tribalism as the biological evidence that it is true. Regardless that no one can show any physical evidence of "hard wires", the myth continues, probably for the same old reason: The financial benefit of some very powerful people.

It is hard to know just who benefits from tribalism. But for sure someone does, otherwise, most adults, would not be so focused on it. I'm not saying someone created it. What I am saying, is that being tribal is a natural, though temporary, way of being. It is a stage in life during which young people figure out how to live life. Being tribal, for a while, was a good thing for me, if for no other reason than I figured out I did not like it.

Being tribal and keeping people tribal, I'm guessing, first benefitted warlords who wanted to increase the size of their tribe so they could conquer other tribes. As they say, if you want to understand most things, including tribalism, just follow the money.

Fast forward to now. I can see the benefits of keeping people stuck at being tribal. Developmentally stuck people are easier to manipulate and control than people who can think critically for themselves. People who are not developmentally stuck are not very popular, and are often attacked by people threatened by the courage it takes to be free of tribes. People who are no longer tribal are often feared and hated because their ways take power and control away from those who benefit from it. This sounds a little conspiratorial, I know. Besides, I am honestly having trouble giving so much credit to a small group of greedy bastards. Regardless of how all this actually works, I am currently 'perspiring' with much success to become such a feared and hated outcast – better than running with the herd and looking up the butts of others, is what I'm thinking.

My intent in this chapter is to share with you my observations and ideas about the people who made up the myth that being tribal is "hard-wired" in all humans. And just to be clear, when they say, "hard-wired", what they mean is, that it is permanent. If being tribal for life includes being racist, tribes in constant conflict with each other, it is a very gloomy picture for the future. I was, therefore, very curious about the people who want us to believe that there is no hope for our sorry, pathetic tribal existence.

I am sure you won't be surprised I have concluded that believers in our "hard-wired" nature are tribal. Their tribe believes that bad behaviours like prejudice, racism, and the like are caused by wires, and they value spreading this belief. As a result, they promote the idea that being tribal is a physically caused way of thinking and behaving that cannot be changed. All their beliefs, values, and actions are requirements of being in their tribe. I don't believe they have any idea that being tribal, and all the negatives that come with it, is a stage in development from which we have the potential to literally escape. The proper way of saying it, I believe, is "grow beyond".

Here is an example of "hard-wired" believer I found without hardly breaking a sweat. Biologist Doug Tallamy was quoted in my local newspaper as saying, "Humans are wired for tribalism, conformity is a sign of belonging". To me, this statement is in the same category as, "She had a nervous breakdown", to which I have learned to respond, "Which nerves broke down? Can you show them to me, and what wonderful machine did you use to see those broken-down old nerves?" As a trained biologist with diplomas on the wall, Dr. Tallamy should be asked the same question. He should be able to show those "wires of tribalism" that he writes about.

At this point, you just might be thinking, "Sally, that's unfair. Surely Dr. Tallamy is speaking figuratively. He doesn't really mean wires". Well, if he didn't mean wires, what did he mean? Since words matter a lot, should we not hold someone with a fancy degree to a standard that can benefit us in our struggle to understand life? I'm thinking, "yes."

Dr. Tallamy is not alone in creating and spreading this myth that being tribal is a hard-wired lifelong condition. Religious people do it all the time. They absolutely, without hesitation or reservation, believe that all humans need to belong. People just don't know it yet, but it is best for them all to belong to a particular, religious tribe. Once they do, that tribe will be their safe place. Belonging to their tribe is a ticket into Heaven, but only if a person is blessed with the 'divine grace' to be accepted into it. Because to be accepted into the religious tribe is a God-given privilege. God must be incredibly generous to us humans with this gift since there are so many religious tribes all around the world.

If you are also thinking right about now, "Just a minute, Sally. You talk about not having a pot-bellied stove to explain what it means to be an addict. Is that not the same as talking about being born with tribal wires?". Well, I suppose it could be, if I was saying we are either born or not with a pot-bellied stove, but I'm not saying that at all. What I am saying is that we get one or not from the environment in which we are raised as infants. In fact, that environment includes the womb in which we develop for nine months. Since we create both environments, it is in our control to create nurturing or harsh ones. And just because someone is poor, oppressed or not well-educated doesn't mean they can't create a nurturing environment for a child. I honestly believe that the creation of addicts can be prevented by virtually anyone. Robert described this so very well in the first book, TWO.

In contrast, the belief that we are "hard-wired" to be tribal for life takes away our power to grow beyond it. The belief justifies being stuck and doing the horrible things tribes do. There is a huge difference in the two ways of explaining how we are. Yes, my pot-bellied stove explanation is a made-up story, but it is a useful story, full of hope, because it explains a serious, worldwide problem that stumps many brilliant, thoughtful, and well-intentioned people. Best of all, the explanation leads to productive action. I'm a good example of that.

I think people like Doug Tallamy make an all too common mistake. They are not careful with the words they use, and as a result, deliver a hopeless message. Being tribal and being social are two very different things. I touched upon this in the second book, "Freedom" and will talk about it more later in this book. In a nutshell, we survived the dangers of the world thanks to those who were more social. By the process known as natural selection, the social survived and the less social, cranky loners did not. So, we have evolved to be naturally social. Well, at least most of us have.

This makes perfect sense. All we have to do is look at our own children. My son, from the get-go, has had a unique personality of his own. It is becoming more pronounced as he gets older and includes liking to be around people, especially other children. There are benefits to him being comfortable in, even preferring, the company of others. We all benefit from it. From the very beginning, the advantage of being social was survival. Some look out for danger when others need to sleep. It is easier to fight off a saber-tooth lion together than alone and far more food can be gathered in a social group in a shorter period of time.

As you read this, please do not make the mistake of thinking that there is a very fine line between being tribal and social. There is not. Being tribal is one distinct stage among other stages in our development. If our development is obstructed, as mine was, we get stuck. Once the obstruction is removed, we move on. I moved on, far on, from being tribal but I am still very much social. What I like the most about being social is that I am free to decide what to believe, I am free to choose what to value and free to decide how to act in situations. If I screw up now, I can no longer claim, "I was following orders". It is my responsibility.

To be social and no longer tribal is not difficult to describe. It feels good. I feel like a grown-up, responsible person, more advanced than when I was tribal, like I am no longer under the direction, actually the control, of others. I am now my own person. I did have many obstacles to overcome in my development but I could never have become this if there were permanent "hard wires" keeping me tribal.

Just to round out this chapter, let me repeat what I have learned from books about this tribal versus social debate. According to people who call themselves 'developmentalists', tribalism is an unavoidable stage in life's journey. It is also a necessary stage at which young people, mostly teenagers, sort out who they are compared to others, where they belong or if they want to belong at all, what they want to believe, what to value and how to behave in different situations. I went through this important process myself. It was not easy, and I can see it would not take much to settle for being controlled by the tribe. I also got stuck because I joined a tribe of drug-using, alcohol-drinking losers. Robert's tribe in the first book, TWO, was not. While he learned important life lessons, figured things out and moved on, because I was always stoned, I did not, and I got stuck.

At this phase of my journey, it is very clear to me that my – our – survival depends on being social, caring about each other no matter what. Being tribal, on the other hand, is just one stage of many on the journey to becoming human. There are no "hard wires" involved, nothing physical holding us prisoner in this tribal-stage, prison cell. Understanding this is the first step to breaking out and making a run for it.

In summary, here I go with another warning. Do let us be more careful with the words we use. Let's all pay attention and select the right word for the message we are trying to get across. Poor Dr. Doug Tallamy, he just used the wrong word, I hope. He said "tribal" when he probably really meant "social". Knowing there are no real wires, I have no problem with being "hard-wired" to be social for life. I have no problem with needing social contact, caring about the welfare of all people, sharing and helping wherever and whenever there is a need. It's just kind of unfortunate that we have to be tribal before we can be fully social.

Chapter 3

INSTEAD OF PROGRESS, WE SETTLE FOR CHANGE

I love clever sayings. I wish I could come up with one of my own. AA has many, virtually one for every troubling situation. When you think about them, however, some sayings are not as clever as they sound. The one that particularly bothers me, and I will explain why in this chapter, is, "People want progress, but they don't like change". Bullshit! Since being abstinent from all intoxicants, what I constantly observe is all that people want is change. They fight progress with all their might.

I am writing this during the Donald Trump administration's ridiculous, fumbling efforts to manage the COVID-19 pandemic, his reaction to losing the election, and the profound outrage in response to the murder of George Floyd by the police. I get that the Republicans are supporting their guy, regardless of how foolish he is, but I don't get how some not-so-foolish people can. My solution to figuring this out, like any puzzle, was to read. As luck would have it, I found just the book. Ezra Klein, a political reporter, wrote, "Why We're Polarized". After reading the whole book, it struck me as really strange that only once did he use the word tribe and only when mentioning another person's book. How can you write a whole book about a nation polarized (split in half) without at least a passing mention of tribalism? I'm guessing he can only see the forest because he is too far away to see all the trees. I am also guessing that this is how his tribe sees the politics that they write about.

Overlooking that Mr. Klein failed to include tribalism in his analysis of American politics, indeed way of life, he did describe many changes that have all taken place without producing progress. Most interesting was how the two political parties, tribes, changed their beliefs, values, and ways of doing things over time. I had no idea – why would I? – that immediately after the Civil War, the Democrats were like the Republicans are now. For example, it was the Democrats who opposed a proposed law to making lynching (almost always of blacks) illegal. Now they are a political party of all races. The Republicans are now mostly white Christian fundamentalists, and they are the ones often accused of being racist.

While these are clearly significant changes, where is the progress? The public murder of George Floyd by paid officials looks very similar to the public lynching of black people with no official interference.

I also learned from reading Mr. Klein, and it makes perfect sense to me, that political tribes care very little about ideas, policies, and how people behave in general. All they care about is winning, beating the other tribe. Many Republicans probably care less how their man thinks and behaves. All that matters is that he can beat the Democrats. The very same goes for the Democrats. When this is what motivates people, ideas, and actions that could lead to progress do not matter. Not much different from sports. Winning is all that matters. Progress has no place in tribalism.

Here is another familiar example of change without progress. When I was young, living my shit life and sometimes going to church, the Catholics taught us kids that eating meat (even a single hot dog) on a Friday would land us in hell forever if we died the next day without confessing our horrible sin. They taught us the same about going to church. If we did not go on a Sunday and died Monday without confessing this other horrible 'mortal' sin, straight to hell forever we would go. Speaking of confession, we had to make sure to tell the priest all our mortal sins in case we suddenly died, like in an accident. As kids, we lived in fear of God and our stoned parents. Nice way to treat children… Not!

All these Catholic rules have now changed. Why is not interesting, nor do I care. The point is that the religious tribal beliefs, values, and ways of doing things change all the time; however, there is no progress. If you want to be in the tribe, you still have to live by their rules. You are still stuck, trapped in this tribal jail cell. I discuss this more in the next chapter, but progress would nurture the developmental potential of people, not scare them with threats of the eternal fires of hell.

Getting back to "Why We Are Polarized", the author only talked about two big groups. Seems to me there are many more groups in the two and outside of the two. Seems to me the whole of America is made up of all sorts of tribes, which means it is a nation stuck developmentally, probably for the same reasons I was stuck. The environment is so hostile that everyone is afraid and looks to their tribe for safety. In the home of the brave and land of the free, most people are forced to be tribal out of fear. Easier to write about two big political groups and their shenanigans than the truth. If the first step in moving forward for us addicts is to admit, take responsibility for our problem, why not the same for a nation? Why not the whole world? I see tribes most everywhere, and so will you if you look carefully, and that truth has to be addressed.

Sometimes, but not often, changing tribes can be a temporarily good thing, but it's never progress. I changed tribes. My friend Ron changed tribes. He went from being a social activist who hated materialistic things, to a conservative who loves his things and the money with which to buy them. No progress, just change.

A great deal has been written about the 12 Steps in anonymous programs. Some of what people write could be interpreted as promoting growth and development. Maturity in thought and action, to be precise. Sadly, however, there is no direct talk in any of the 12-Step literature about growth and development. Instead, there is much talk of God and a higher power. Seven of the 12 steps focus in on one or the other. This tribal belief prevents many people from participating in the fellowship that provides the external source of heat they need. They cannot get their head around a father doing something good, let alone a made-up one in the sky. For them, tragic, past experiences were ruled by nasty fathers. Incidentally, as an aside, the very word 'alcoholic' in AA prevents many addicts from getting the external heat they require. They feel excluded just because they prefer their drug in a form other than liquid.

Sure, I get that there are tribes that are more socially acceptable than others. That's why we celebrate when a drug user becomes an abstinent, hard-working, minimum wage-earning slob. Harsh words but true. Exchanging tribes, in every case, including mine, initially, is for sure a change, but no progress at all. That's why I had to find a way to leave the tribe, to progress, without giving up the benefits of the external heat-providing fellowship.

The first step for me was easy. I can't take credit for being naturally curious, but it sure comes in handy. So, I read and read all sorts of stuff about personal growth and how tribes prevent people from making progress in ways they don't even realize. I read about people who protect the status quo by holding us back, and how people are punished for their independent ideas and actions that break the rules of their tribe. As I was doing all this reading, I got excited about what I was learning and shared the insights with friends. The response I got was a whole new experience for me. I discovered that people read for three reasons, all of which include some element of pleasure.

Especially my AA friends, but also others, only read stuff that reinforces what they already know. They don't mind the repetition. In fact, they deliberately search it out. Having others say the same things in different ways is very comforting. The more people believe the same things, value the same things and behave as they do, the better they like it. They have no interest in different ideas or ways of doing things. Their battle cry seems to be: "Don't confuse me with facts. My mind is already made up".

Then I met a bunch of people who respond to everything they read, see or hear with destructive criticism. Everybody to them is "stupid, lying or incompetent". Calling names makes them think they are better than everyone else. They are easy to pick out by their superior, sanctimonious attitude. To quote the legendary rocker, Ronnie Hawkins, they are "legends in their own mind". Facts and credible information just roll off them like water off a duck's back. Of course, they never offer a better or even a different way. They can't. They got nothing. All they got is their tribal rule of being destructively critical.

I don't much like the company of these two groups of people. At best, they provide short-term, cheap entertainment.

The third group is altogether different. Sadly, they are few, but when I find one of them, I latch on like a swamp leech to a bare ankle. This group of people read, watch, listen to and constantly search for different, out-of-their-comfort- zone information. They love to have their mind messed with, challenged and disrupted. They especially love figuring things out, solving problems big or small. Don't confuse them with 'opinionators'. Opinions are like you know what, everyone has one. These are the people who make conclusions, formulations, based on good information. They have learned what good information looks like and can easily recognize junk. They are an absolute joy to be around.

Based on these observations, I concluded that just being around such people was no longer going to be good enough for me. I decided to 'perspire' to become one of them. And becoming one of them, I concluded, was not just changing tribes; it was going to be huge progress for a long-stuck person like me. Finally, I was heading to that next stage of reasoning and behaving, a place where more than my tribe matters. A place where the interests of all people are combined into one, and everyone benefits.

Just the idea of eventually getting there gave me the excited energy I needed to get started and to stick with it.

Chapter 4
THE PRODIGAL SON

In the early days of my abstinence, I seriously explored the possible benefits of religion. Since I went, when I did go, to a Catholic elementary and secondary school, and there is a priest in my AA group, it was not so difficult for me to often go to Sunday church services. Besides, I always thought of church as a quiet, peaceful place to sort out ideas and practice being in the present. I also really like the incense the priest uses on special occasions.

One Sunday, my AA priest-friend, always hustling for a dollar, used his sermon about the Prodigal Son to sell reproduction pictures of Rembrandt's painting of it – the son in front of the father and his brother lurking behind in the shadows. I did not understand why at the time, but the story and the picture had a huge impact on me. The story bounced around in my head because I could not make sense of it. I kind of knew there was an important message buried in it but not the one my priest-friend was sending. Sadly, I did not have the money to buy the picture the 'good father' was hawking, but I decided to as soon as I could afford it. You will understand why, once I explain what I believe is the story's real message.

I will start my explanation with a related discovery. By definition, each and every tribe has all the answers to everything, knows best and knows more than any other tribe. Tribe members do not think, they know. What they cannot explain, they know by faith – faith, meaning there is no need for evidence or reason to believe that something is true. For a tribe to exist and survive this is necessary. Who would want to belong to a tribe that does not have all the answers to everything (except the week's winning lottery number)? Surely, no one would even think of joining such a tribe.

The confidence tribes – especially the religious ones – have in their beliefs comes from the written word. Well, as I discovered easily, most of what is important was not originally written in the Queen's English. Most of the important ideas and lessons about religion, science, the human condition, and so on, were originally written in another language. Much of what we read about that kind of stuff, therefore, is translated. However, as the saying goes, "Much is lost in the translation". Lost because the people doing the translation have their own agenda, axe to grind, and they are betting you won't know that their translation is a distortion of what the original author intended.

Two brief examples will make the point. I once read a little book, when I was going through my emotional problems, written by someone who spoke the language of the famous Sigmund Freud. He said the English/American version distorted the meaning of Freud's ideas to fit into the belief system of its American translators. He gave many convincing examples.

Then there are all sorts of books written by religious scholars who similarly make the point that translations have seriously distorted Jesus's message over hundreds of years to suit the purpose of those doing the work at the time. My favourite book is "Jesus Before Christianity", by Alfred Nolan. He, too, makes the point very well that "much is lost (distorted) in the translation".

All this relates to the many interpretations of the story of the Prodigal Son. While each is slightly different, the basic theme of the stories is very similar. I will describe, the best I can, the tribal belief behind the message. Incidentally, you can consult "Mr. Google" for yourself to see Rembrandt's painting and read brief statements about what it means.

Simply, the Prodigal (which means reckless and wasteful) Son asks his father for his inheritance, not wanting to wait until the old guy dies off. He gets it and in short order, true to his name, squanders the wealth on wine, women and song. Of course, he ends up penniless. He then apologetically crawls back to his father, who immediately forgives him. Not only does the father forgive the guy, but he throws a big, elaborate party to celebrate his return and apology. The older brother, who did all the right things, resents all the fuss made over his loser brother and refuses to participate in the celebration.

The common lesson to be learned from this story, is that the father, like the Heavenly Father, God, has endless mercy and will forgive anything and everything. All you have to do is ask. The worse sinner you are, the bigger will be the celebration and the rejoicing when you ask for forgiveness. In contrast, the older resentful brother is made out to be bad because he is jealous of his loser brother being fussed over.

Trying to get my head around this biblical lesson, the best I could come up with is: 'Knock yourself out, sin, and screw up as much as you can. Just make sure you take the time to ask for forgiveness, and then you can go out and do it all over again'.

Really? That is the point of the story?

What about the older brother? Is it bad that he is jealous, or is it bad that he expects special treatment for doing what he is supposed to do? Or is it both? This big lesson-story makes no sense to my very practical mind. It seems to be some kind of tribal thinking that those outside the tribe are not meant to understand.

Or is the story of the prodigal son just another excellent example of biased, agenda-driven, distorted translation of a perfectly good lesson? I believe it is. However, there is a different and very important lesson in it for all of us. Not the lame, Kool-Aid one the religious tribe wants us to drink.

This is what I believe the story means: screwing up and asking for forgiveness is really about admitting, accepting responsibility for, and shouting out, "I have a problem!". It is like the 1st Step in all the 12-Step programs. Coming to accept what is real is something to rejoice about because without that 1st Step, there is no moving forward, no addressing or getting a life-destructive problem under control. A problem cannot be addressed, controlled or fixed if it is not seen, recognized or acknowledged. Without these things happening, the problem does not exist, although the harm it causes sure does.

So, I'm hoping you are asking, what is the problem to which the son is admitting and for which he is taking responsibility?

I believe the inheritance the son squandered is the gift of developmental potential with which he was (we all are) born, to become a responsible, capable adult. And here it gets a little tricky. At first, his father, and later he, disrespected, failed to honour the gift. When the prodigal son was a child, his father, as a parent, was responsible for bringing his son's potential to life. Since his father failed to do so, as an adult (in age not maturity), it became the prodigal son's responsibility to bring to life the gift of potential. I failed in this, too, and have watched countless others do likewise. That is the problem the prodigal son takes responsibility for in the story. The beauty, the reason for celebration, is that once a problem is acknowledged, the doors open wide for moving forward. Since getting and staying abstinent from all intoxicants, that is exactly what I have been doing. Like the theme of my second book, 'Freedom', I am growing up, taking responsibility for what it means to be an addict, although I certainly did not ask to be made one, and doing what I must to stay abstinent. All good reasons to celebrate, which we do faithfully each year on my anniversary of getting abstinent.

I will be the first to admit that I have not read even close to everything written about the Prodigal Son story. I'm pretty sure, however, that no one has interpreted the story as I have. Obviously, I'm no genius and certainly not the first to recognize that we are all born with the gift of cognitive, and many other, developmental potentials. In the next chapter I will get into this. Here, I just want to trouble you, as I am troubled, to wonder why few people recognize, let alone talk about how the gifts of developmental potentials are wasted, and how people choose instead to settle for the false comforts offered by tribal beliefs, values and behaviours.

I'm not sure what to make of the older brother, except that he was expecting praise and a celebration for doing what he is supposed to do. That is just so wrong. It is as wrong as making heroes out of people for doing the job they signed up to do. What is heroic about treating sick people if that is your job? What is so heroic about putting out fires, rescuing stupid people who fall into a gorge or arresting bad guys if it is your job to do so? If it's not your job, if you were not trained for it, if you are afraid to do what has to be done but do it anyway, now that is heroic. Doing the job you signed up for and doing what you were trained to do, not so much. So, the older brother, I believe, is as screwed-up as the other one but he does not recognize it.

I don't want to bore you by going on but I can't believe such an important message about wasting the precious gifts of developmental potential versus doing what you are supposed to do were buried in the Prodigal Son story. I can, however, believe that the main message was distorted simply to recruit members to the various religious tribes. Sweet! It's ok to screw up, as long as you ask for forgiveness before you die. That is one powerful sales pitch that has and continues to work well for most religious tribes. I tried this deal, even before knowing the story. Screwing up and expecting others to pick up the pieces when you say, "I'm so sorry", can quickly wear thin by the time you are potty trained. So, I learned.

Legend has it that when asked why he wore several different religious symbols on his chain, Elvis Presley said: "In case there is something to this religious stuff, when I'm at the Pearly Gates, I don't want to be kept out because of a technicality." I like his thinking. Similarly, in case there is something to this bearded heavenly father person who grants (or doesn't) wishes (prayers), I don't want to piss off the Big Guy by ignoring (wasting) this precious gift of developmental potential. And if there is not, I still don't want to waste it for my own sake. At the end, I want to be proud of what I have done with it.

Chapter 5

NIHIL SUB SOLE NOVUM: NOTHING NEW UNDER THE SUN

The title of this chapter is one of the few phrases I remember from high school Latin class – which no one even takes any more or even knows what Latin is. No matter. What matters is that there is a great deal of truth to the saying. With very few exceptions, there are no revolutionary, earth- shattering, new ideas out there. Ideas just get repackaged or are buried, only to come to life once in a while, only to be buried again.

The first reason for writing this chapter, therefore, is to show you that humanity's developmental potential being obstructed at the tribal stage was identified at least three thousand years ago. Our habits of reasoning and as a result, how we behave just following the previous primitive ways children, criminals, most addicts, and addicted addicts reason is nothing new. The second reason, and what bothers me most, is that we have done nothing about it. To this day, very few people even recognize it to be a problem. As you well know by now, if a problem is not acknowledged, it remains a problem, nothing is done about it. Oh, there have been a lot of changes over the years, mostly of the technology kind but no real progress in how we get along as humans. I believe all our prejudice, racism and cruelty to each other are caused by most of the world's population being tribal. So, stop thinking there was a time when 'things were better'. There was never, ever such a time. Sad, is it not?

Let me begin by describing how I discovered information on this topic. The story begins with me poking around a bookstore. Quite by chance, as often happens, I came upon two very interesting books. The first is full of pictures and dates when people lived and what they wrote about. The title is, "The Philosophy Book: Big Ideas Simply Explained". How could a curious person like me pass up buying such a book? At the time, I was struggling with religious tribalism, the idea of a "Sky Father" responding or not to my begging (prayers); so I just had to buy the second book I found, "Jesus Before Christianity".

A significant part of my growing up and getting-well routine is meditation. It is a Buddhist practice, so I now know some things about the teachings of the Buddha. I looked him up in the philosophy book and found that almost a hundred years before him (600 B.C.), Laozi, in China, talked about living in harmony with nature as the path to a well-balanced life. Does that not sound like the indigenous definition of spirituality and my conclusion that, as an addict without a pot-bellied stove, living in harmony means getting that external source of heat regularly for the rest of my life? About fifty years later (550 B.C.), Confucius, who most everybody has heard of, said that virtue (or in today's language, principled reasoning and behaviour) can be cultivated by anyone. To me, that sounds very much like deliberately activating our gift of cognitive developmental potential, leaving behind the horrible ways of all tribes. Then, around the same time (480 B.C.), in India, the Buddha said our developmental potential is obstructed by our constant pursuit of short-term gratifications (probably the sex, drugs, and rock and roll of his time). The goal of life, he said, is to think for ourselves. The following is attributed to him:

"Believe nothing, no matter where you read it, or who said it, unless it agrees with your own reason."

The Buddha also said:

"The mind is everything. What you think, you become."

Assuming the translation is not distorted, does this sound all too familiar? Is he saying, don't let others (the tribe) tell you what to believe, value and how to behave? "Develop your own ability to reason, and then you decide," is the message I'm getting from this dude.

Throughout history people have gotten themselves into all kinds of trouble for that sort of talk. The philosopher Socrates is another one. In Greece (469 B.C.), he was charged with corrupting the minds of young men by teaching them how to think. Not what to think but how to think. For his troubles, he was given two choices: go into exile from his homeland forever or drink the poison hemlock and die. He chose the hemlock.

There were others getting into trouble for talking about our developmental potential, like John the Baptist but most familiar to us is his cousin, Jesus of Nazareth. More has been written about the teachings of Jesus than probably anyone else's. Since he spoke Aramaic, everything known about what He had to say, His message, is a translation. And, by now, you all know to be suspicious of translations. Those doing it often distort the original message to suit their purpose or agenda. That's what most of that book, "Jesus Before Christianity", is about.

I would love to take you through all the translation distortions described in the book. Instead, however, I will focus on the main message, as I described above.

In the book, the author, Albert Nolan, makes the point that at the time, Jesus would have understood the perverted, sinful (developmentally stuck) ways of the world to be due to Satan (status-quo protectors, those who obstruct development) being in charge. He would have seen Satan's power (the consequences of obstructing the human, developmental potential) evident in the suffering of the poor and oppressed as well as in the hypocrisy of both religious and government leaders (the very same as now), whom He would have seen as Satan's (the 1% establishment's) puppets.

Nolan believes the accurate translation of Jesus's message is that if people reasoned better and acted accordingly, Satan's (establishment, status-quo protectors) influence would be replaced by God's (activated, cognitive developmental potential) influence. The reign of evil would then be replaced by a reign of goodness. Goodness, Nolan interprets from the message, is more powerful than evil and therefore would triumph over Satan's influence here on earth. I like that message because not only does it make sense to me but it also says I have the power, we all have the power, to make our lives better here on earth. Nolan says the Kingdom of God is here, not up in the sky somewhere. There is nothing in the message of Jesus, Nolan also says, of putting up with suffering here on earth because we will be rewarded for it by being allowed into heaven when we die. That message looks to me and to Nolan as a translation distortion to benefit those getting richer by the minute from the suffering of the poor and oppressed.

If you're thinking Nolan and I are also just choosing to translate the message of Jesus to suit our purpose, you are wrong. The distorted translation is just stupid. Suffer here, make a small group of people very rich, and you will be rewarded with heavenly paradise when you die. If that was really the message, the establishment, status-quo protectors would have loved Jesus. They would have crowned him king. But that was not his message. His message threatened those in power, and we all know what happened to Jesus. He, too, was silenced for his efforts to get us unstuck from being tribal.

Seems to me, most people who want to mess with the status-quo end up badly. Thankfully, the world does not run out of them.

Six hundred years after the crucifixion of Jesus, the next troublemaker for the establishment was the Prophet Muhammad. His message was beyond similar. It was almost identical, but also eventually distorted in every which way. Just observe the strange rules by which Moslems are required to live – no more or less strange than what was, and still is, required by Christian tribes.

A few hundred years later, many philosophers talked about our obstructed cognitive developmental potential. The German philosopher, Immanuel Kant, in the year 1700, urged people to think for themselves and placed a great deal of weight on our potential ability to figure things out. A hundred years later, in the year 1803, Ralph Waldo Emerson also talked about living in harmony. He told people to reject conformity and traditional authority and replace it with developing their personal integrity and the ability to think for themselves. Every person, said Emerson, has the power (potential) to shape his or her destiny (future), a message that, I hope by now is starting to sound very familiar.

I will end my examples of almost identical messages by referencing a couple of the best-known prophets of our own time. The Reverend Martin Luther King, Jr. expressed the message with marvellous beauty. If you have not read his, "I Have a Dream", get it, print it, frame it, hang it, and read it frequently. Not a week goes by that I don't read it at least once. Then there is John Lennon's, "Imagine". It is just as beautiful a message. I listen to it also at least once a week.

Like many before them, their ideas about our potential were dangerous to the establishment, status-quo protectors. The fundamental religious crowd considered their ideas to be those of Satan, and you can imagine what the white supremacists thought of Dr. King's vision of the future. Needless to say, both paid with their lives for daring to identify and speak about our inborn potential and for daring to urge us to develop it. There is a part of me that thinks all the war zone, siege-like conditions of the past and present have, and continue to be, orchestrated to stop progress by obstructing our developmental potential. But that's just me being paranoid, a condition I 'caught' during my brief, nasty dance with psychiatry. In reality, because we are stuck at being tribal, bad shit just happens a lot, all the time.

Let me summarize then what I learned by being curious, searching and reading. The idea is not at all new that our miserable human existence (don't forget, I'm writing this during COVID-19, Black Lives Matter global outrage after the murder of George Floyd, and the reign of Donald J. Trump) has been, and continues to be, caused by our obstructed cognitive developmental potential and how we behave as a result. It is old stuff talked about in all sorts of ways. Some ways are to the point and others are lost in the translation. Regardless, the message is clear: This is our human problem, and *it needs to be fixed*.

So, you may be wondering, why has there been no big-time recognition of this horrible problem? First of all, it is not because the philosophers and prophets are wrong. I believe the reason is that the very nature of the problem is the problem. No committed, Kool-Aid guzzling tribe member is going to think that being developmentally stuck is real, let alone a problem. They will have no clue because their tribal rules value neither being curious nor reading, listening to or exploring ideas different from theirs. When I was a kid, we were told by our nun and priest teachers that reading the Jehovah Witness publication, The Watchtower, was a sin. For the same reason, I was afraid to go to the Jewish Community Centre just around the corner with my neighbourhood friends. I have many more examples of people stubbornly staying in their familiar comfort zone, strictly following their tribal rules, but these should do. As a result, they have no idea how harmful to them their tribalism is.

I now firmly believe that you cannot fix tribalism and the bad that comes with it like racism, prejudice, and hate for different others because they are different - that's what tribalism is. However, we can get past and outgrow tribalism. I am very optimistic about our gift of potential to do so. I am, because I am actually doing it. I am outgrowing my need for the approval of the tribe. I am outgrowing my fear of reasoning, thinking for myself. If a former big time screw-up like me can do it, so can you. All you need is a little discomfort with the way things are to motivate you, to release your curiosity to search and discover. I'm slowly learning there is nothing scary about being on the outside moving forward. You should try it. You just might like it.

Chapter 6
THE BENEFITS AND COST OF TRIBALISM

As I learned in my first-year college Introduction to Psychology class, all creatures, especially humans, repeat doing what gives them pleasure. Even if something makes no sense or just seems plain bizarre to you, for that person, the result of what they are doing is rewarding and therefore the action will be repeated. This, I have observed, also applies to being in a tribe. The bigger, more powerful and popular the tribe, the better are the rewards for being in it.

By now, hopefully, I am getting across that being social is in our natural make-up, whereas being tribal is a temporary phase or stage in our growing up. Unfortunately, it is a phase at which most people on this planet get stuck. In this chapter, I want to share with you why I believe (which is better than think) being developmentally stuck is so rewarding and then at what cost the rewards come.

The first place to start is the obituaries in the newspaper. I read them most days and commonly find: "Suddenly called home to meet his Saviour," "Entered into God's heavenly care," "Entered eternal life," "Our Lord and Saviour called her home," "Entered into the loving arms of Jesus," "The Lord called her to Himself," "Is joining predeceased parents, spouse or child," and many other similar pleasing beliefs about what happens after death. Curiously, however, I am seeing less of these beliefs as the parents of my generation die. While fewer people seem to express these tribal beliefs, for many, the beliefs remain comforting while they grieve the death of a loved one. They must be very grateful to their tribe for teaching them these beliefs. The teaching by religious tribes, that suffering here on earth or dying in a 'holy war' is rewarded in the afterlife must also be very comforting. As must-be beliefs that the tribe is doing God's work and their work is therefore noble. The almost-religious Masonic tribe members tell me that they are all about promoting what is best in their members but not through "financial or mercenary gain". However, they don't say how. Perhaps they do it by having their members memorise lots of stuff and keep secrets. I don't know. Then there are the Jehovah Witnesses, who are apparently comforted by regularly knocking on my door, trying to get me to join up so I can get to heaven. Although they believe there are only a limited number of available seats there.

Political and sport fanatics all seem to benefit from tribe membership in two important ways. First, membership defines who they are. It gives them a real comforting sense of identity. Next, winning, beating the opposing political candidate or sport team is the ultimate pleasure for them. Just check out the destructive riots after a candidate, or especially a sports team, wins or loses.

Another likely benefit to all tribe members includes the comfort of not having to think, especially critically. Faith without reason or logic is good enough. "Don't confuse me with facts or with ideas different from mine. My tribe has already taken care of telling me what to believe, value, and how to behave. The bigger my tribe, the better we must be. I am extremely comforted that we all think the same. It would be even better if we could get more members or if everyone on earth joined our tribe." These are the attitudes I hear, not in so many words, from my friends who are tribe members.

I wonder for example, if everyone joined the same tribe, would that be the end of tribalism? Would that mean that we would all get past the stage of tribalism? I don't believe so. First of all, it will never happen, and even if it did, tribes would arise within the tribe. This has already happened, and continues to on a smaller scale. For example, political tribes have tribes within their tribes, the same as religious tribes that have within their tribes liberals, conservatives and fundamentalists. The answer to our human misery, therefore, is not to get everyone to join and stay in the same tribe. The answer is to get unstuck from the tribal stage in our developmental journey and to fully use the gift of potential with which we are all born.

Getting back to the 12-Step tribes and the reference to God in seven of the steps. It must be so comforting to believe that there is a "Heavenly Sky Father" to look after us just for the begging (praying) and in ways our earthly father (parents) never could. Especially comforting about all the 12-Step programs, at least it seemed to me while begging for help with abstinence from all intoxicants, is the belief that being an addict is an illness or disease, that it is a medical problem. Therefore, it is not a family, community or socially-caused problem. Never mind that in 1988, the Supreme Court of the US of A refused to grant 'alcoholism' the status of a disease. Also, never mind that good, hard science cannot find observable or measurable organic causes for addiction or madness. The collective tribal mind is nevertheless made up that addiction is a disease and therefore a medical problem. This framework is an indestructible fortress that cannot be broken into by different or better perspectives.

I could go on, but won't, about just how comforting and rewarding tribal membership is, and as a result, why we human beings have been stuck at this stage of our developmental potential since the beginning of time.

The many comforts, however, come at a horrible price. It is a price I believe to be infinitely greater than the puny, emotional rewards of tribalism. Greater, because seeing and suffering the consequences don't rely on faith; the consequences are there to be seen, and we all experience them daily.

The beliefs, values, and expected behaviours of any tribal membership are not harmless. Even the ones that seem harmless are, in fact, harmful. Let me start by describing the obvious well-known ones. Some of us, as children, learned at Sunday School or some other indoctrination into the Christian, religious tribe, about the Crusades of the Christian Holy Wars against the Muslims. Many had to die so that a few could benefit from those tribal wars. Fast forward to World War I, "the war to end all wars," shortly followed by World War II. In these wars, literally millions had to die to benefit those who prosper from humans killing each other. Nations, ethnic groups of all kinds, killing one another was, and always will be, about tribalism. Just yesterday, I saw on the news a white supremist confronting an opposing tribe member in Charlottetown, USA. This vicious man is nothing more or less than a horrible example of a person acting on the beliefs and values of his tribe. So it goes on, and as someone once said, "Far more evil acts have been committed by groups than by individuals". I say, therefore, the focus should be less on the individual vicious asshole and more on the tribe to which he belongs, that he represents and that gives him the identity he clearly values.

"My tribe is not like that. My tribe is a good tribe. We only do good deeds," you are probably thinking right now. Even if that was true, which it cannot be, the very fact that you are a tribe member makes you part of the problem that is responsible for human misery since forever. The very nature of tribes means none can be a good, harmless one. And just being stuck at the tribal stage makes it so very easy to slide a stage back to an even more primitive, "what's in it for me?" "what can I get away with?" I want my needs immediately satisfied, way of thinking, and then acting accordingly. There is nothing good about being tribal, even for a teenage mall-brat.

I am writing this amid the global COVID-19 epidemic and watching with curious horror what is happening to our old people housed in extended care facilities. It seems to me that how most people get old, and how we treat the old, is all laid out by tribal beliefs, values and prescribed ways of treating the old – which is not so well at all. Then I got to thinking about my future. Do I want to live that long? Do I want to be trapped in my body having to rely on someone else to even wipe my bum? Of course not… do you? How did we get to this cultural, tribal practice of keeping people alive so long, only to warehouse them where they exist in misery until they die?

How we gradually got to treating old people this way, at least in the industrialised world, is another huge example of at what cost comforting tribal beliefs come. I am talking about the religiously required tribal belief that, "life is precious". No, it's not! It sure did not look like that to me especially during my shit life growing up at home, and while using. There was nothing precious about my life or the lives of others I hung out with on the streets. In fact, when someone died of an overdose, we all felt a sense of relief the person was finally delivered from unbearable misery. We had similar feelings when one of the girls got an abortion after an unwanted pregnancy.

The unborn was saved, rescued from a life of misery - not unlike the misery experienced by me and every other addict without a pot-bellied stove, before being born and then in the lousy environment of their upbringing. Whereas I got to saying, "That is enough", got straight, and started to grow up, far more people never do and suffer all their lives. I know many people like this, and their life sure doesn't look "precious" to me.

Why then, do most (especially religious) people sell and require purchase of the belief that "Life is precious"? There are probably many reasons, one of them being, "The more in our tribe, the better for us". With more comes greater power, influence, control, safety, and for some, wealth.

The benefit of getting and staying abstinent from all intoxicants is to experience life completely differently. The difference is in quality. That is what is precious. That is what I want and will work very hard to hang on to. When time takes what belongs to it from my body and mind and the quality of my life slips away, I will not settle for quantity. Why would I want to? Why do so many, even among the religious tribes, hang on when they believe that eternal heaven and their Sky Father is waiting for them on the other side? This makes absolutely no sense to me, but then I have no faith, and I no longer need to be in a tribe. I have, however, the ability to reason with my mind.

So, instead of using our financial resources and our great scientific minds to keep us alive longer and longer – one guy, I read, is aiming for a hundred and fifty years - we should be investing our resources into improving the quality of everyone's life. Now, this would really mess with the status quo and would require thinking that is far above and beyond the tribal mentality most of the world is so stuck on. So what? We should do it anyway.

I am reluctant to touch on this next tribal issue because I am sure to offend many. The topic has to do with my indigenous AA buddies. By now, we should know well about the destruction of Indigenous peoples and culture by European settlers and religious missionaries. While much of importance has been written about what was done to them, it is of little use when it comes to figuring out how to fix it now. From getting to know my indigenous AA buddies, I believe they are no different from any addict, including myself. Like all addicts, they have no pot-bellied stove, and they came by that like the rest of us. Their mother's pregnancy was horrible as were all of our mothers', and the environment they were exposed to during the formative years was shit, just like ours. It matters little that it all started with the Europeans and continues to this day because of legal, medical, political, and social tribal views. To stop what has been going on for generations (and will surely continue), the damage to their culture has to be undone. Whereas they have a culture to restore, we other addicts for the most part have no such thing. We have to start from scratch, which requires a huge disruption of the status quo. Still, however, we as individuals of all colours, race, and nationality get and stay abstinent. In doing so, we break the generational pattern by being better persons to each other and by being better parents to our children. I just wish we could do a better job of preventing the making of addicts around the globe.

The lesson for me in all of this, is that we all have to be conscious about the tribal perspective from which we are interpreting and trying to solve a problem. I cannot imagine how tribal ways could be of any value, unless the goal is to advance the tribe's size, influence and power. While curious, I am not particularly brilliant. I was nevertheless able to figure out that being tribal is a very bad way to be. I decided to stop being part of the problem and to become part of the solution. The most important, the most significant thing I did was to consciously, deliberately, with focused purpose, activate the gift of developmental potential with which I was born.

Having said all of this, I want to make it perfectly clear, as a recently abstinent addict, I am well aware of my status as a "human becoming". Therefore, I do not want to insult or in any way disrespect what has gone on before. The tribal beliefs of religious and 12-Step programs, at times, have probably served some purpose. Perhaps, at various times in the past that was the best people could do to explain their world and experiences. But this is now, and some of us are a lot savvier than were even the founders of AA. What I'm saying is, let's hang on to the vital benefits of the AA fellowship and in the interest of progress; let's stop begging for stuff (praying) and reach inside to better use what we already have.

Since getting abstinent and working toward growing up, I am discovering some important things about being a "human becoming". What brings me great comfort, real quality to my life, is my ability to solve problems. Instead of begging (praying) for favours from a "Heavenly Sky Father" (or mother), I look within myself for the strength, courage, grit, and smarts to cope with or to solve problems. They are there, I just have to stubbornly look for them. Being able to count on myself instead of something or someone else is incredibly comforting. If I can do it, why can't you?

If for a moment, however, I let myself buy into tribal beliefs about a "Heavenly Sky Father" and beg (pray) for good health, success, wisdom or any of the many things people beg for, there just might be a huge downside to that. The Heavenly Sky Father just might be insulted by the begging; insulted, because the begging implies He or She made mistakes. The begging suggests, "You did not give me enough. You did not foresee what I would need, so now I am pointing out Your mistakes and begging You to fix them". Well, just because your tribe believes in and values praying (begging) to a "Heavenly Sky Father", do you really want to insult Him in this way? How about honouring Him by believing that He knows everything, including what you would ever need. If you did that, you would be at the same place as I am, except you would have gotten there in a different way. No matter, as long as we end up there together. Now that would be progress!

Last but by no means least, while I don't know but sure hope so, there must be some religion-based group that focuses on spirituality, living in harmony and developing the potential with which we are all born. If you find one, get involved! If there is none to be found, think about starting one yourself.

Chapter 7

REALITY INSTEAD OF PLATITUDES

I need to start this chapter with defining the word "platitude". According to Mr. Webster, it means overused, irrational, exaggerated, unwarranted phrase (saying). In other words, "bullshit".

I have grown to hate platitudes. By using them we are without knowing or intending protecting the status quo. By using them we are denying our global problem of obstructed developmental potential.

I may really be going out on a limb here, but the use of platitudes is so common and, I believe, harmful that, at the very least, some lively discussion about it is needed. Instead of throwing about unjustified phrases or slogans about ourselves and others to create false pride in our tribes, we would all be better off working to be real.

Before going any further, let me be perfectly clear. I am not talking about Muhammad Ali, who declared, "I am the greatest". For sure he was and for me, could do no wrong. Seriously, the point I want to make is that there was no harm done by his schtick, whereas much harm is done by the exaggerated claims of others. Many waste great opportunities for progress by resorting to platitudes when being real is called for.

An easy place to start examining platitudes is with politicians. They like slogans and often use them to define who they are and what they intend to do. All political tribes use them at one time or another. Slogans are a problem however, when they are also platitudes. Presidential candidate Barack Obama shouting, "Yes, we can" is still vivid in my memory. I think, don't know for sure, he was saying the American people have the ability to make progress. A catchy slogan but as a platitude about the American people, not justified. Worse yet, he probably believed the slogan and did not realize he had made it a platitude. At least, I hope so. Otherwise, he was being phony. Better if he had acknowledged the reality that his country is in great trouble and there is much difficult work to be done, starting with removing the systemic obstacles blocking their cognitive, developmental potential. I get it, no one talks like that and no one would understand such talk, but any talk that focused on potential rather than the platitude of nonexistent ability would have been much better.

Particularly upsetting to me is the phrase Congressman Elijah Cummings is best known for: "We are better than that". He was reacting to the nasty, illegal political shenanigans of, I think, a Trump lawyer. A well-intentioned, thoughtful man tragically wasted his great influence on a platitude. How could he have done that? Why did he say that? Again, I would like to think he actually believed what he said. Perhaps he was also misguided by the belief that people rise to the occasion of becoming better than they are if challenged or given the opportunity. That was never my experience personally or when watching others. Whenever I was challenged beyond my capabilities, especially when using, I just gave up. The same as my son when I tell him, "It's easy" when it's not. He just gives up. So, I learned to tell him, "This is hard, but you can do it. I'll teach you how". Then he hangs in there and learns how. Based on my narrow but big experiences, I believe the good Congressman's great influence would have been better used spreading reality. Just a little tweaking would have made a world of difference: "We have the potential to be better than that". Now, that would have started something long overdue, activating in people their gift of cognitive developmental potential, asleep due to thousands of years of obstruction. I get it. No one talks like that and that would not have made a good slogan to be remembered by. But it sure would have started an interesting and important conversation. Perhaps the conversation would even have produced progress. What a shame it never happened.

Another tribal platitude I touched on before is, "Life is precious", which is similar to, "Lives matter". Both are platitudes because they are not naturally real. We live and die by circumstance. We all have what is called an inalienable right to the life we have. That means nature gives it and only nature can take it away, like the blues song lyric, "That's just a natural fact". What nature does not give to the lives we have is quality. I believe therefore, we should be saying, "Quality of life matters" and then go after that. It does not make a good slogan, but it sure gets to the real cause of our miserable existence. The world population is approaching eight billion and from what I can see, most people have very little, if any, quality to their lives. Is just being alive good enough? Should we just shut up and be thankful to be alive? Or, am I allowed to go for some quality to my life and not be held back in all sorts of ways, including the feel-good, tribal platitudes that life is precious by well-intentioned but poorly informed people?

Then there is President Donald J. Trump's ridiculous slogan-platitude, "Make America Great Again". The slogan is pure nonsense, just like the idea of rehabilitating criminals or addicts like me. I have known both, and I would not want a single one returned to some previous way of being. Like me, they all need to grow up. They all need to move forward, not back. My question to now-former President Trump and his tribe is: "When was America great?" Was it great before the Civil War, when fortunes were made on the backs of African and indentured slaves? Was it great during the Depression or the Vietnam War? Perhaps Donald Trump and his tribe think it was great when black people were publicly lynched for the pleasure of white onlookers, when schools were segregated, and black people could not drink out of a water fountain because of the colour of their skin? Oh, no, wait. America was great when his father was able to build the fortune Trump inherited and made bigger by doing all sorts of nasty things like his father, but even better. Going back to those times would be good for Mr. Trump and the tribe to which he belongs. Not so much for the others, including all the tribes put together, what people call society. So, Mr. Trump's reality-based platitude works for him and a few others but no one else.

Telling children they are great, calling people great also are silly platitudes. No one is great. No nation, culture, religion or race of people is great. It is what we do that is great and we all have the potential to constantly do great things. If you think about it, greatness is in the doing NOT in the being. And the doing comes from thinking. However, if the thinking is obstructed, if it is stuck at being tribal, while things change pretty regularly, progress in the human condition seldom, if ever, occurs.

Since I have been abstinent from all intoxicants, I am learning to be a competent, empathically-nurturing parent. All that means is that I know my son is not an extension of me; I value that he is his own person and love him for it. As a result, my son is developing the potential with which he was born. Fancy that. By watching and listening, I am learning a great deal about how he and his friends the same age think and behave. Their ability to pretend, to fantasize is something to behold. It is a marvelous ability in children but not so much in adults. As adults, we need to face and deal with reality. Platitudes do not help, and our tribe's requirement that we rely on them, even if only as a catchy slogan, does way more harm than good.

Instead of having irrational, tribal beliefs or faith, such as that our suffering on earth will be rewarded in the afterlife, let us all face reality and let us all start doing things here and now. In my own way, I have started. For example, there are real benefits to being curious, reading all sorts of things, especially unfamiliar, new stuff, discovering all sorts of new ideas, figuring out new, better ways of interpreting experiences and global events, and most of all, becoming my own person, not what a tribe says I should be. All this started when I recognised and acknowledged the problem, that being tribal belongs to a teenager's stage of thinking and behaving. While teenagers suffer greatly at this stage, adults stuck there suffer even more. Being stuck prevents adults from doing important adult things like raising well-adjusted, high-functioning children, looking after others in need, and most importantly, becoming spiritual humans. As you will remember, being spiritual means living in harmony with each other and with our environment.

Let's lose the platitudes and let's make it real. The real is that we are far from the "human becomings" for which we have the potential, and we are far from living in harmony with each other and our environment. We continue to settle for tribal religions, politics, and all sorts of meaningless platitudes and identities instead of pursuing real spirituality. Making progress, based on past and current events, will continue to be difficult with many tribal obstacles to overcome. However, it is very doable. I have started doing it, and so can you, so we can all start doing it together.

Chapter 8

WHAT WILL IT TAKE?

I end my story in the first book of four in this trilogy with, "Hi, I'm Sally, and I'm an addict". I had to go through a lot of shit for a long time to get to that point but I did get there. Ever since, as I have repeated over and over, my life has been moving forward. The changes I am making now are mostly progressive. They are not just window dressing as for example, switching from one tribe to another. At first, that is exactly what I was doing but no more.

In this chapter, I want to share my ideas about what it would take for the whole (at least most) of the world to get to the point of "No more... that is enough". In chapter five, I named just a few of many who tell us our problem is that we are developmentally stuck. What they all had to say, and what I have experienced certainly leaves no doubt that indeed we are stuck. Similarly, there is no doubt that the obstruction of our cognitive developmental potential and how we behave as a result is our own doing. What no one has said so far, however, is that we are stuck because we are stuck. Since some, including myself, can get unstuck, the lesson for me and you is that it is possible.

So, you say some catastrophe or major negative event will do it, much like hitting rock bottom did for me. Not necessarily. I am writing this during the COVID-19 pandemic and during the global outrage about the murder of George Floyd by one police officer while three more looked on. The global outrage is already calming down and people are increasingly less uptight about the chances of getting the virus. So, the impact of these horrible events, like the impact of all previous horrible events, just fades away. World events, regardless of how horrible, just do not get us past the denial, platitudes and tribal rule that dominate our lives. The evidence is too overwhelming that regardless of how horrible the event, conditions slowly but surely return to what they were before… tribal.

Let's hammer away at this reality a little more. Did World War I, "the war to end all wars," stop World War II from happening? No! Tribalism in the form of nationalism raged on. The horrors continued until two atomic bombs put a temporary stop to at least the war. Not for long, however. The Korean War, the so-called peacekeeping mission of television series 'MASH' fame, broke out followed by the Vietnam War. The tribal killings continue in the Middle East, Africa and by religious terrorists everywhere else across this globe. It does not matter how you spin what was, and is, going on; we remain nothing more than tribes fighting and killing each other. Grim, is it not? But so true.

Let's think, then, about racism, specifically racially motivated violence, mostly by white people against mostly black people. But there are many other forms of it all over the world. For me, racism looks very much like tribalism. If I'm correct, which I believe I am, then there is no fixing racism, just like there is no fixing tribalism.

They are the same thing, sometimes more and sometimes less so but always together. The protests, riots, the burning of neighbourhoods always bring about some change but never any progress. If there was progress, racism would have long ago faded away into the past. Sadly, so far, it has not. Since forever, we have been stuck at being tribal, and racism is just one part of the huge price we pay for it.

Some people say, and I have certainly seen and lived it, that progress only comes from shit piling up, like the straw that breaks the camel's back. Perhaps, the last killing of a black man or woman or a war here and there will do it. But the wars in which millions have and continue to die, and the constant murder of black people, the cause of global outrage, are just never enough to finally break that camel's back and move us forward. While science says we are all more similar than dissimilar, and philosophers say we all have the same right to life that can not be taken away from us, we nevertheless continue to live in disharmony by gathering in tribes and behaving like we are told. Not necessarily blindly following orders, like Nazi war criminals, but with equal lack of awareness, acting out that which is required for membership in a tribe.

Perhaps, we need to use the word "tribe" more often. Perhaps we need to have our noses rubbed in the shit tribalism is so that we can no longer ignore its stench and impact on our species. I was about to say human race but thought better of it because most of us have not even started on developing our potential to be human becomings.

Despite everything, despite us being stuck at the tribal stage of development, I am 'optimistically hopeful'.

My hopeful optimism is based on real experience: mine. I saw, questioned and thought about tribalism in the 12-Step programs. It was not a complex puzzle beyond my capability to understand and do something about. Having tribes based on what way people like to get stoned, I decided, is stupid. Then I discovered it is not stupid. It is something worse. It is being tribal. Next, I learned being tribal is being developmentally stuck. Being developmentally stuck, I then learned, is better than being stupid because you can get unstuck but you can't get "unstupid". At the end of all of this figuring, I decided I did not want to be stuck. That is the theme of my second book, Freedom, which is about getting developmentally unstuck and starting to grow up.

Since getting developmentally unstuck was good for me, I also decided that my son was not going to follow in my user-addict footsteps for a minute. That while being tribal is an unavoidable stage in development, he was never going to linger, and for sure, never going to get stuck there. So, I bought books on parenting and promised myself to create for that boy of mine an environment that was all about turning on, giving life to, the gift of developmental potential with which he, like all children, was born. Doing all this, being a competent 'empathically-nurturing' parent is work both physically and mentally but does it ever pay off!

Instead of hoping that my son would have the curiosity that got me developmentally unstuck, I orchestrated an environment for him way different from the one to which I was exposed at his age. Because he is doing so well, as a result of my deliberate, self-educated parenting abilities, I came to the conclusion that no big event, or the piling up of shit, is going to get us, most of the world, developmentally unstuck. To start, therefore, we must first individually grow out of it. Even nasty little teenagers running around in their shopping-mall tribes sometimes grow out of it. As stuck adults, we can do the same. The challenge is to discover the formula for dissolving the glue that keeps us stuck, and I am well on the way to doing exactly that.

So, I say again, finally getting the world unstuck after thousands of years can only begin with the individual. Like with me, it has to start with a commitment to ourselves and then to our children to do everything we can to bring to life their gifts of developmental potential. The everything must include the school environment to which we have to entrust them at a pretty young age. We, the parents of our precious children, have to get involved with the educational system. We have to because the evidence is that primary and secondary schooling have done very little, if anything, to prevent our children from getting stuck. It has to change, and it will not do so on its own. Certainly, no developmentally-stuck directors of education, teachers or politicians are going to do anything more than implement superficial changes in this or that. They probably instinctively avoid progress at all costs. Don't forget, an activated developmental potential is a huge threat to the status quo. It will be up to us individual, developmentally unstuck parents, to gradually bring about progress in our current, oppressive educational system to one that is passionate about activating the gift all our children are born with, their developmental potential. Of course, they will also have to continue teaching our children how to read, write, and count.

The answer to what will it take to get us unstuck, therefore, is: me and you. No wise person, no prophet, no philosopher, no politician, no catastrophic event, not even thousands of years of piled up shit is going to do it. It will take us individuals, perhaps inspired by some from the past and present, to honour the gift of developmental potential by nurturing it so it can flourish. So, let's not waste time complaining, especially on the various social media channels. Instead, start doing things that stimulate and challenge your mind. It will take getting unstuck developmentally to realize just how stuck you have been. It will take getting unstuck for you to realize you do not ever want your child to get stuck at being tribal or worse, the even more primitive stage before that.

I cannot end this chapter about "What will it take?" without once again getting into the touchy topic of religion, one of the most visible of all the tribes. My AA priest-friend, the one hustling the framed Rembrandt picture of the Prodigal Son, once asked, "What will it take to get more young people into the church pews?" At the time, I was lost for ideas. I was doing my own sorting of beliefs. Happily, I am no longer as lost, and it is a shame he is long retired. So, here is my answer for you other priests asking the same question.

Lose the images. Lose the statues. Lose the pictures. And lose the focus on the guy on the cross. Hang on to the guy's original, undistorted message because that is where it's at. Instead of requiring specific beliefs, values, and behaviours, instead of requiring faith in all things that are without evidence, focus on spirituality. Focus on learning how we can live in harmony with our essence as human becomings with our various developmental potentials. Focus on developing the cognitive potential in us that we require to live in harmony with others and our environment. If your priestly purpose is to save people, save them from the disharmony that is being developmentally stuck at tribalism. Nothing sustainably good has ever come from it. A lot to ask, I know but at the very least, do a little less of the traditional and do more of what life requires of us. If all you priests at least try this different focus, eventually there may be only standing room left in your churches.

In closing this chapter, I want to say that I do a great many things, some good, some not so good but for sure, I no longer think or act like a fool. My hopeful optimism has a rock-solid foundation. It is based on real events. Events I have experienced, seen, and read about. I am unstuck, and my son will never be stuck like many people I have had the privilege of personally knowing. Most of all, my hopeful optimism is based on my observation that what it takes not to be stuck is not all that difficult. What is required is for you to decide that tribalism is bad and that you do not want to be stuck there. Once you decide that, you will begin your journey forward and happily continue as a "human becoming".

That is what it will take!

Chapter 9

BEING SOCIAL WITHOUT BEING TRIBAL

This last chapter is the thirty-sixth I have written in this four-book trilogy about addiction. You would think it would be the easiest and shortest of them all to write. All I need to conclude with is that being tribal is horrible, so stop it. But many others have already said this for thousands of years, and it still goes on. It still goes on despite tribalism being the cause of probably most, if not every, atrocity by humans against one another and against Mother Nature. While tribalism is an unavoidable stage in the sequence of human development, there is virtually nothing good to say about it. Just ask any teen going through it or reflect on how horrible your experience was as a tribal teen, way back when. Yet most of humanity continues to be stuck there. What makes this sad reality especially horrible is that it does not have to be this way.

And that is where this last chapter becomes difficult to write. I can't just say: "Follow my example and you, too, can leave the tribe behind." It is not that easy. If it was easy, people would have listened to the Buddha and many others, and we would behave completely differently than we do now. And please, do not confuse technological advances with human progress. The two are completely different. Technology has not made us better. It has lightened our burden in some areas of life and has provided some cheap entertainment. But technology cannot make us think and behave at higher levels. In fact, technology can be, and often is, a curse. It is the newest obstacle to the activation of our gift of developmental potential. Telecommunication technology is the means by which we can now stay constantly connected to our tribe and the tribe's influence over our lives. Medical technology has been extending our lives but so what? Often the extended life is not a life of quality worth living. It is a silent, miserable existence waiting for the end to come. Sadly, most of us have watched a loved one go through this and, as a result, welcome their death as a deliverance. Another so-called benefit of medical technology is that for the most part, we are healthier now than ever before. This would be progress if the health came with a quality of life. Often it does not. I know many physically healthy but very miserable people. Again, I say, life is not precious. Quality of life is precious, and many on this planet have very little of it.

So, let's not confuse technological changes with progress. On the surface, what we see is incredibly different than what was there just a hundred years ago. Underneath the surface, the human condition, however, remains the same. As I was writing this a few weeks after the murder of George Floyd, I heard today a police officer shot another black man in the back seven times as he was walking, not even running, away from him. Despite our local and global outrage about Floyd's murder, tribal behaviour goes on and on.

If you are willing and committed to getting unstuck and do what it takes to make certain your children never get stuck at being tribal, you need to know what being unstuck looks like. You also need to know what it looks like to be social as opposed to being tribal. Knowing what the two look like makes it easier to go after and easier to know when you are achieving it. My breaking off with tribalism started with the realization that 12-Step programs are unnecessarily tribal.

Stuck at being tribal, my brain was on pause because of the false comfort that comes with it. Then by chance, thinking about experiences or reading something like this, the pause button got turned off. That's what happened to me when I thought about the difference between being an alcoholic and a pothead. Without the pause button on, I could clearly see… no difference. We are all addicts without pot-bellied stoves, and that's all that matters.

To get you started then, this is what it looks like to be nontribal. Someone with the highest form of development, what the books describe as being a 'principled person', to me is the ultimate best at being social. To start, you should know that being principled does not necessarily require a great deal of thinking. Getting there does but not being there. A principled-person's life is pretty straight forward. There is no "me" and "them". There are no enemies to conquer and there are no campaigns to sign up new people to a tribe. What there is, is a focus on the good that comes when we are all in this together. Everyone is treated with the same respect, regardless of who they are and regardless of the circumstances. Like the three musketeers, "All for one and one for all". Pretty simple stuff when you get there. Not so much during the getting there.

The big difference between being tribal and principled is that the tribe does your thinking and all you have to do is follow the tribe's rules. A principled person has had to do a great deal of thinking to choose his or her way in life. The choice is not a set of rules like the Ten Commandments, it is a way of being all the time. It is always living by The Golden Rule: "Do unto others as you would have them do unto you". To live this way requires being aware that the other person may have their own unique, emotional reaction to a situation. This is called having empathy, which by the way, no one is born with, you learn it. It's never too late. I learned it later in life because I knew I had to. To live this way also requires a constant, almost automatic awareness of how you would like to be treated. The two put together is what a super-social, a principled-person's thinking and behaving looks like.

Being social –heading toward being principled – does not mean you stop doing things, stop going to certain places or stop seeing certain people. I still go to my AA meetings because without the external heat provided by the fellowship, I will freeze to death… I will go back to using. I also attend church services and often visit with my retired AA priest-friend. My frame of mind, however, when I do these things is very different from when I was stuck at being tribal.

So, I can be very social without being tribal. It looks the same, but it is very different.

Let me explain more. I still enjoy the culture of many tribes. There is nothing better when it comes to food than sampling the cuisine of any and all tribes. In that respect, I am a mini Anthony Bourdain, the late, world-traveling chef. I also love tribal fashions and fashion shows. For me, it's art in use, and it's wonderful. Most tribe-specific music also is wonderful, although about some, I can only say, "Very interesting". Dance is the same, especially the Irish Riverdance people. Then there are people of different tribes. Hanging out, getting to know people from all different kinds of tribes is one of my most favourite things to do. I love listening to their stories, what they believe and value, and how they do things. Sometimes they frighten me, but I get past it because of my curiosity, my need to know what makes others tick. In a nutshell, I am never in any no-brains- required comfort zone. And I have no need to be. For sure, if you followed me around for a while, you would seldom see me hanging-out with the same people. I am on the move, enjoying all that life has to offer.

As a mother, I am interested to know mothers from different tribes. I want to know how they think about parenting, how they actually parent and, most of all, why they think and do as they do. I also want to know about their successes and their failures as parents, spouses, employees, and employers. Being curious is a wonderful way to be. It takes me to many places and is a significant source of quality to my life. I really like becoming human.

That is what it looks like to be social without being tribal. The other difference is that I am not accepting offers, enticements or encouragements to drink any Kool-Aid. I decide what to believe, value and how to behave. As a result, and based on experience, I often change my mind about things. Hopefully, each time I do this the change I make is progress toward my goal of being a social, principled person. Having left and out-grown the tribe, there is nothing still or rigid about me. It is this phase in my journey that makes me my own person, using my mind to investigate, interpret and then decide for myself what's what.

I should say here that, most of all, I love the company of a principled, super- social person. Sadly, I meet few but the few I meet are a delight to be around.

I don't want to give the impression that my current life is some Walt Disney World fantasy. It is far from it. It is for sure difficult, full of problems to be solved. If it's not one thing, it's always something else. But solving puzzles, figuring out how the pieces fit together by myself, can be a great deal of fun and can be very rewarding. Let's also not forget this life I have now is all because of the external heat I regularly get from the fellowship of my AA group. That is why I still go to AA meetings regularly and often also attend church services. But my frame of mind, my reasons for doing these things is very different from before. No one would know that I am no longer tribal, because I am social. I now love them all, which was not so much the case when I was tribal. There is another big difference: Along with all intoxicants, I have also given up 'faith'. Now, I use my ability to reason and then choose for myself. Some AA stuff I choose to hang on to. Others, like the idea of alcoholism as something, a disease or illness, I choose to let go.

You may be thinking by now: "How do I comfort myself without tribal faith when bad things happen as they always do in life?" That is a very important question because it has to do with how a recently-abstinent addict accomplishes self-care without getting high or resorting to child-like fantasies such as, heaven is waiting for me, or for begging, a "Sky Father" will look after me. The answer is that I do very well at looking out for myself.

For example, when it comes to coping with death, I remember one of the first things I learned in high school physics class. While I was not a very good student because I was using in those days, I do remember a very simple law of nature: energy cannot be created or destroyed. It can only be changed from one state to another, like water into ice, steam or split into its atoms, hydrogen, and oxygen. Without making this into a physics class, my point is that since I am essentially energy, I have always been, and I always will be. In what form is not important. This reason-based belief is good enough for me. The actor Shirley

McLean said something very similar. I think it got her into some hot water with religious tribes. If the same happens to me, I don't mind being in that company (notice I did not say tribe).

The US presidential election now done, as I write this, provides a great example of what a social decision for whom you vote looks like. If you are tribal, you simply want your tribe to win, regardless of the person, regardless of the person's character, beliefs, values, policies or behaviour. You simply want the enemy, the other tribe, to lose and your tribe to win. Now, if you are social, decisions are based exactly on what a tribal person ignores. Your social, principled decision will be based on the candidate's character, beliefs, values, policies and behaviours, anticipated by how that person behaved previously. I predicted the people of the US would vote tribally. Many did on both sides of the divide. I can only hope some did not and that progress, not only change, is on the horizon.

That we are cognitive developmentally stuck because our gift of potential is systemically obstructed by status-quo protectors is the bad news. The good news is that we can do something about it because there are no genes, no hard wires, no imbalanced chemicals responsible for it. The obstacles are of our own creation. Therefore, since we do it, we can stop doing it.

I want to, but hesitate to, give examples of principled, super-social famous individuals. For example, I can't give you the unifying liberator from British colonial rule, Mohandas Gandhi, because some claim he was racist. Since he was certainly not tribal, I don't see how he could have been racist. Nevertheless, I also can't give you the peaceful, highly accomplished, assassinated, civil rights national hero, Reverend Martin Luther King, Jr. because many say he was an "immoral" womanizer. He was certainly not immoral, in fact he sounded and acted like a very principled super-social person. Nevertheless, I am sure the maliciously critical would find lots to criticize about any "grown up" responsible and principled public figure. So, it's probably best to stay away from examples of well-known people and just hang on to the idea that many people have activated their cognitive developmental potential and behave accordingly. You probably know such people in your circle of friends. I certainly know a few and knowing them makes me wish there were a lot more.

To summarize then, curiosity got me to question the tribal status quo. Instead of curiosity killing me, like that troublesome cat, it freed me to pursue becoming a principled, social human. Curiosity revealed what it looks like to be social and how to recognize super examples of it. Now you, too, have the same knowledge. I believe generations before did not have as much knowledge as we have now, and that is why mostly only changes occurred and seldom progress.

I know, and now you know, where you want to get to, and now you also know what it looks like when you get there. If others have gotten there, I believe we can also get there. If I accomplish my reason for writing this book, you will set your sights on leaving the tribe for being social, eventually becoming a principled, "human becoming". We can then join forces and become a formidable opposition to the establishment protectors of the status quo. Once we are free of the tribe and get to being social, we can then work toward making sure each future generation will struggle less and quickly pass through that unavoidable tribal stage on their way to becoming what the gift of developmental potential has given them.

REFLECTIONS

INTRODUCTION

There is nothing more powerful than a good story so I have heard and personally experienced many times. Telling a well-crafted story relevant to the presenting problem, like the story of Sally, was a constant intervention strategy during my almost fifty-year career as a demonologist (psychotherapist, for those of you who have not read the previous books). Hopefully, the story of Sally's journey and lived experiences was a good one. Hopefully, the story has touched you emotionally, intellectually, and at your very core sufficiently for a significant life-lesson to emerge. My intent, clearly, was not to dazzle you with academic jargon, convoluted language or countless references embellished by pages of footnotes. My intent was to make especially the language, Sally's words, accessible. Aside from a possible academic promotion, complex, abstract, ideas serve no good purpose. I am, in fact, a little embarrassed to have 'perspired' to acquire and show off exactly that academic skill, albeit a long time ago. Now, I resent just a little that I believed it was expected of me, and that I actually acted on that belief.

I do not, however, mean these comments to be disparaging toward scholarship and the abilities that come with such acclaim. Steven

Pinker, author of "Enlightenment Now", Jared Diamond, of "Collapse", David H. Freeman, of "Wrong", Ezra Klein, of "Why We're Polarized" and Gabor Mate, of "In the Realm of Hungry Ghosts", are just a very select few of many whose skill in writing I admire. Despite my above comment, I really do covet and even tried to emulate the elegance with which they write some ten years ago in, "Because We Can We Must". For my efforts, I garnered comments like, "Lots of words", "Too dense", "The ideas are too complex" and, my personal favourite, "Too many big words", of which no one could readily give an example, even when enticed with a crisp hundred dollar bill. I often wonder if the above-mentioned authors have received similar reactions to their scholarly works. Certainly not from me, which is excellent if I am their intended audience. But to me and my kind, they are artist-scholars we have learned to appreciate. We buy and actually read their books. In contrast, the message in these four books is not aimed at a select few. The message is aimed literally at a global audience, so I had to make the language as accessible as possible.

Given my past 'perspirational' ill-placed writing ambitions, it was therefore, a great challenge to find a voice for Sally that is believable and that I could consistently write in throughout this trilogy. By the end of this project, one Oxford Thesaurus is now a well-worn, dog-eared book. I hope my effort to write accessibly is at least of some success and will inspire others, who believe they have something to say, to do likewise.

I won't insult you with false modesty. Obviously, I believe I have something to say about this insidious, global problem of addiction and two other phenomena debilitating the world: the harm caused by prescribed psychopharmacological drugs – the theme of the third book and tribalism, the cause of all atrocities past and present – the theme of this book.

The lesson I hope you take away from these four stories is that progress is possible. It has always been possible but obstructed by status-quo protectors. To this day, in spite of the voices of many to which I have added mine, few recognize the human problem to be tribalism, an unavoidable, cognitive developmental stage perspective which we should all glide through if not for the fact that being stuck there keeps us there.

Fortunately, being stuck at tribalism need no longer be a life sentence for successive generations. The added insights in this book, I hope, will serve as the tipping point for most to do what, so far, a select few have accomplished –specifically, get unstuck. There are many who have, and I have personally known several Sallys who activated their gift of cognitive developmental potential and got unstuck. My own good fortune was that I never got stuck, probably because no one wanted me in their tribe. Sometimes it pays to be uncomfortably different from most others.

If this last book touches you, if the ideas resonate with you, you then need to act. You have to follow Sally's example, starting with setting your curiosity on fire. Then, you need to agitate, where and when you can, for a plan to redesign all levels of our woefully misguided and ill-informed educational system. All schools, everywhere, need to be places where the activation of children's gift of cognitive developmental potential is paramount because children who grow up to understand and embrace principles also behave accordingly. That would not be change, that would be long overdue progress.

A WORKING HYPOTHESIS

While writing this fourth book, I had the good fortune of finding and reading David H. Freedman's 2010 book, "Wrong". The subtitle is, "Why Experts Keep Failing Us – And How to Know When Not to Trust Them". As you can imagine, the title, let alone the content, got me seriously thinking. What if I'm wrong, what if there is no merit to my psychosocial (person in the context of their environment) unified theory-perspective? What if alcoholism is a real thing? What if being addicted is a disease, an illness not caused by dysfunctional parenting repeated intergenerationally? What if the answer to all our problems is some chemical concoction prescribed by a psychiatrist to sedate us until we no longer care about what bothers us? What if tribalism is a hard-wired biological reality of our existence and all we need is to destroy all the other tribes until there is only one left? The right tribe of course. Finally, what if there is a Sistine Chapel-like, bearded, personified God, whom we should constantly beg for favours because that is what He expects of us if we want to live forever in Heaven? Of course, I could go on, but I won't, hoping that the point is made.

Beyond Addiction: Sally Discovers How to Think for Herself

My first response is to acknowledge that in this universe there are few, if any, absolutes. No one is privy to the "truth" and there are probably no absolute "truths" out there to be had. What I have, what this and the previous three books are, are working hypotheses. This is the best I've got, and I believe the best there is until some contradictory or additional information makes me modify, alter or otherwise improve my current thinking. This is the very reason I genuinely invite one and all to present alternative working hypotheses if you disagree with mine. Just to be clear, this is not an invitation for malicious criticism, like "too many words" or "not believable". Anyone, especially angry tribal people, can, and do, maliciously criticize all things without the faintest idea of what would constitute an alternative constructive strategy, idea or hypothesis.

My second response is like Freedman's when he asked the same of himself. Like his, my working hypothesis has no mention of faith and ideology, both of which are unfounded, irrational beliefs. My working hypothesis is based on observation, things that can be seen, measured qualitatively and quantitatively. My working hypothesis is then an explanation of what I observe and live. My working hypothesis is also in part a synthesis of other hypotheses, although no other person I know of has so far come up with even a similar formulation to mine.

If there are similar, working hypotheses to mine, if my formulations have already been thought of and are published, you would be quite correct to conclude I am also just expressing the beliefs, values, and behaviours of a tribe – my tribe of 'psychosociologists'. That would be a valid conclusion deserving a response. The fact that there is no one else in my assumed tribe is part of the answer, but it is insufficient because I could be in the process of creating and recruiting members for one. The other part of the answer is that I am far from starting or recruiting members for a new or existing tribe. I am, in fact, advocating for independent thought, the activation of the gift of cognitive developmental potential, the pursuit of principled reasoning and the according behaviour. My vision is that of a global population in which the majority reason and act as principled individuals, not as tribe members whose singular purpose is to guard and maintain the status quo that defines them.

Ultimately, however, you are the judge of my ideas and whether I am just advocating for the creation of yet another tribe. Hopefully, using the criteria for a reasonable hypothesis and feasible actions that emanate from it, you will at the very least decide whether or not it is possible to achieve long, overdue progress if we act now to get unstuck.

COMPETITION

Human beings have engaged in some form of competitive play since the beginning of recorded time. We praise and value competitiveness, encourage and socialize our children to it. The rationalizations for being competitive are endless. We rationalize that team sports teach cooperation only to venerate the 'superstars' who single-handedly score and win games. Most importantly, we believe that cooperative play among children is the same as competitively playing a sport. It is not. One teaches children to get along, the other to beat or conquer the other tribe.

Of course, there is no harm in a child or adult challenging him or herself to be the best at an activity. The harm is when there is competition with others. The competition requires players to be tribal, and makes fanatics out of those who watch modern day gladiators do battle. The team fans or fans of a competitor (fanatics) take great delight in the misfortunes of opposing players, especially when they lose to their preferred competitor. The worse the loss, the better. These competitive so-called sports do not bring out the best in us. The "we against them" sport mentality reinforces and perpetuates tribalism in its worst manifestations. European football hooliganism is a good example, riots and vandalism when a team wins or loses is another, and my personal most disliked is the primitive war cry, "We won!"

Fair warning therefore is required. As our developing sociability leaves tribalism in the dust, you would not be mistaken to anticipate a progressive decline in our conflictual behaviour. Expect the first casualty to be fanaticism, like the ugly hooliganism so prevalent in Europe and, equally ugly, team logos painted on flabby, naked male bodies in North America. Next, will be the decline in exorbitant ticket prices that prey on the stagnated, developmental perspective of the majority. Hopefully, we will eventually and finally see the end of modern-day gladiator battles not to the death but to the physical and mental ruination of the participants. I can only hope.

Political tribalism is no better than competitive team and individual sports. Politics also is all about winning, which is accomplished primarily by beating a vilified enemy. Policies, ideas, and proposed initiatives matter not to political tribes. All that matters is beating, conquering the feared enemy. Whether the fear is real or imagined does not matter. What matters is winning, being dominant over the other.

This is the very essence of tribalism, fear, and being dominant over the feared other. No wonder the global majority is developmentally stuck, given the fear mongering in which every tribe engages about one or all other tribes. It is a shame that the current and past antiracism protestors do not realize that their outrage is really about the harm caused by tribalism, expressed as: racism, misogyny, genocide, war, brutality, subjugation, oppression, deprivation, modern slavery, human trafficking, minimum wage, the involuntary intoxication of emotionally troubled people with prescribed drugs, the privatisation of prisons, the forced labour of prisoners, and every other indignity you can think of perpetrated by one group onto another.

THE INDIGENOUS CANADIAN EXPERIENCE

At first, I was reluctant to write this piece. I am far from an authority or even sufficiently knowledgeable about the Indigenous experience with addiction. My resolve to write it grew, however, because I am confident in my knowledge concerning the impact of environmental conditions on a fetus and child during the early, formative years. I understand how addicts are created, and I believe it to be a cross-cultural reality; no different here, there or anywhere else. I do not for a minute discount the importance of cultural differences. They matter a great deal. Our understanding of the differences is the means by which we relate to people from different cultures. Therefore, cultural differences must be understood and the knowledge applied with skilled sensitivity. However, the structure underlying the cultural differences among the people of the world is the same. The story of Sally and Robert in the first book, "TWO", plays out in every nook and cranny across this world, including among the Indigenous peoples of Canada.

On recommendation while writing this book, I read Harold R. Johnson's Canadian bestseller, "Firewater: How Alcohol Is Killing My

People (and Yours)". It was an interesting and disturbing read by the end of which I had only learned the obvious: *That the systemic violent abuse of Indigenous Canadians has to stop.* As well, according to Johnson, Indigenous peoples "have to change the story that we tell ourselves about ourselves and about alcohol".

Easier said than done, otherwise it would have happened already. But there is a lesson to be learned from Johnson's work, and it has to do with tribalism. It has to do with the perspective from which Johnson writes.

By way of a very brief summary that does not do justice to the book, the first thing to know is that the author is an Indigenous lawyer, a prosecutor in fact, who flies into remote areas with a team, including a judge, to dispense justice. Useful to know, because it leads to a working hypothesis that his perspective is one indoctrinated by his tribe of legal professionals, specifically lawyers.

Johnson's approach to the Indigenous problem with alcohol confirms the working hypothesis. His writing is that of a lawyer, providing evidence upon evidence as to how the European occupiers of the land, in the most egregious ways, systematically set out to wipe out his people. In an appendix, he provides the entire legal treaty between "Her Majesty the Queen and the Plains and Wood Cree Indians and Other Tribes of Indians". Included in the treaty, at the request of the Indigenous, is a ban on alcohol on all the lands. Subsequently, however, the Canadian Bill of Rights declared such a ban unconstitutional. This, then, changed the Indian Act, leaving it to each reserve to ban or not, alcohol. To his legalistic perspective, Johnson adds a number of conundrums: "Are we drunk because we are poor or are we poor because we are drunk? Do we drink because we have nothing to do or do we have nothing to do because we drink?"

Interesting questions, but not relevant to the problem of intergenerationally-created addicts who abuse many substances, one of which happens to be alcohol. These questions are a parallel theme to his legalistic perspective. Specifically, he persistently draws attention to the legalized, structural violence against Canada's Indigenous peoples. To his credit, he acknowledges that, we do not make change in the world by preaching and passing laws" but then expects it to occur as a product of changing "the story that we tell ourselves about ourselves and about alcohol".

Curiously, Johnson makes no mention of Indigenous people's use of other intoxicating substances such as marijuana, glue or gasoline sniffing and other street-obtained illegal drugs. Perhaps, references to the use and abuse of other intoxicants would diminish the historical significance alcohol has had on some, not all, Indigenous people. But by choosing to ignore the other substances, Johnson inadvertently gives credence to the belief that alcoholism is something more than a substance some addicts prefer, exclusively. By falling into this trap of legal tribal thinking, he fails to see the real issue. Namely, that the problem to be solved and prevented is the intergenerational creation of addicts who invariably become addicted. Giving significance or importance to what substance the addicts become addicted to is a misguided, legal tribal focus which leads to virtually nowhere.

As a clinician with almost fifty years of experience, I find it difficult to believe that the Europeans trading alcohol for fur made Indigenous trappers 'crazy drunks' on the spot. For sure, if alcohol was a completely foreign substance, its effect was significant on the novice, Indigenous consumer. But even then, since there is no evidence that Indigenous people genetically do not process alcohol well, like some Asians, there is no cause to assign any particular importance to it, other than its relative availability.

The critically relevant point is the European policy about the Indigenous people their explorers or settlers encountered. It was to assimilate but preferably destroy them. It happened in Mexico, Central and South America, the Pacific Islands, and all other places invaded by a foreign tribe. By the time we get to the picture of the "drunken Indian" from the settlers and traders, already much harm had been done to them. The stress and trauma perpetrated on some was creating addict children, children without pot-bellied stoves like the Sallys all over the world.

Perhaps Johnson's, "We have to change the story", when defined fully, entails the people recovering the dignity, culture, way of life, and parenting practices traumatically taken away from them through systemic, violent genocide.

Assuming this expanded definition is correct still leaves us wondering how what is required can be accomplished. The "how" becomes even more of a challenge, considering Johnson's own statement, "We do not make change in the world by preaching and passing laws". Certainly, a great deal of preaching and tinkering with laws has gone on, producing superficial change but absolutely no progress.

Consistent with my purpose for writing this series of books, the first task in addressing any problem is understanding it. The Indigenous experience and the experience the world over of people who have been made addicts is the same as Sally's experience described in the first book, TWO. Persistently perpetrated trauma and/or stress seriously and permanently compromises the fetus during the nine-month gestation period and the developmental tasks of children in the early formative years. The trauma and/or stress to the child comes through the trauma and/or stress to the primary caretaker parent, who is mostly the mother. In the case of Indigenous people, it started with the European policy cited above and continues with the various oppressions so well chronicled by Johnson. In no time at all, the problem became intergenerationally perpetuated. Addict parents were and continue to make addict children who invariably become addicted.

As for all addicts, the fellowship produced by the external heat of 12-Step programs works just as well for Indigenous people as it does for all others without a pot-bellied stove. AA meetings are common on many reserves, even those in remote locations. I believe the challenge of preventing, reversing the damage done to many, if not all, Indigenous people is as onerous as it is for the general population, albeit with additional obstacles to overcome.

For example, in Canada, there are many reserves without drinkable water, adequate, nutritious food supply, and basic medical care. The first task, therefore, is to ensure the availability of basic, life necessities to every Indigenous person and community. Then, simultaneously, with focused, deliberate purpose, activating every Indigenous child's gift of cognitive developmental potential has to begin. As in all other cultures, this task is best accomplished through the education system, one that is mindful of the particular people's culture, traditions, teachings, and practices. While developing school systems focused on the activation of all children's cognitive developmental potential in a culturally relevant curriculum is certainly an onerous undertaking, it is very doable. The evidence to support this position is formidable. If it were not, I would not have spent my time, energy, and personal resources to write this four-book trilogy.

Of course, this, like all topics, can be made into a far more complex issue if one is so inclined. This inclination, when indulged, leads to more studies, investigations, reports, and second opinions, the end result of which is a delay in doing what needs to be done. When that happens, the status quo is maintained and the protectors of it have once again succeeded. I believe this has been going on with the Canadian Indigenous problem, as it has with the global problem of addiction in general.

STRUCTURE AND CONTENT

In chapters three and eight, I make a very important distinction between change and progress. My experience is that this is something no one thinks about, and the idea baffles them. No wonder then, that they almost always ask for a description of it… what does progress look like? … is their response to the distinction. I suspect unawareness of the distinction is just another instance of the status-quo protectors at work, making sure we settle for change without knowing that what is required is progress and the change that comes with it. A brief discussion is then in order, focusing only on the key elements.

To make the idea as clear as possible, I will present "change" as content and "progress" as structure. Content is what we see. Content is the things which make our various tribes distinct. Content is the tribe's aesthetics, belief systems, customs, child-rearing practices, the spices used in cooking, the foods eaten, and the colours preferred for painting houses or when making tribe-specific costumes. Often content is appropriated by members of other tribes. Who on earth does not like and regularly eat pizza? Content is also historical.

Gladiators in the Roman Coliseum are now replaced by Monday night football players giving each other concussions and quality-of-life debilitating, physical and mental injuries.

Content is the things we don't mind altering. At first blush we resist, but after a little persuasion, we accept it often simply to make ourselves feel good that we are doing something in lieu of knowing what else to do.

In contrast to content changes, progress entails modification in structure, that which is not directly visible, like the insides of a building covered up by design, wall board, and brick. In the context of these books, transitioning from a tribal, reference-group cognitive developmental stage perspective and behaving accordingly, to the next cognitive developmental stage is an alteration in structure. The structure of reasoning changes because the focus shifts from pleasing tribe members to becoming part of the diverse, social mosaic of the geographic region in which the person lives.

This content and structure distinction is cross-cultural. That is why there are tribes everywhere, and why there are developmentally stuck tribal people behaving badly everywhere. The cause and form of trauma (content) to a pregnant mother can be as different as day and night but the effect (structure) of being bathed in cortisol for nine months is the same for every unborn child. Similarly, the adverse environment on an impoverished remote Canadian Indigenous reserve is very different from a Middle East Syrian refugee camp. Both represent content. The devastating, long-term effect (structure) on the children, however, is the same. Addicts are thus made regardless of the vast content differences by which the harm is done.

Hopefully then, this brief discussion of a pretty complex idea will serve to ensure that you will no longer confuse change with progress.

Most importantly, I hope you will not settle for window dressing, superficial, reactive change. I hope you will demand progress and will settle for nothing less.

HISTORY OF DRUG AND ALCOHOL USE

In chapter five, Sally discovers that there is nothing new under the sun – NIHIL SUB SOLE NOVUM. So, please let us not pretend there is. Like from the platitudes in chapter seven, also nothing good comes from pretending. "Let's make it real", as the lyrics of the old, blues song implore us to do. Let's stick with what we can measure and know about from reliable sources. The utopian Shangri La only existed in the 1920s fantasy of some Hollywood film maker.

In this spirit, then let us make the history of drug use real. Let us not pretend that life in the undiscovered North, Central and South America was some idyllic utopian world. There were tribes just like everywhere else. Tribes fought each other for dominance, survival, material gain, to make slave labourers out of captured enemies, and at times to have a ready supply of sacrificial virgins to offer to the gods.

Tobacco was a crop of North America, and cocaine was grown and consumed in South America. Herbal hallucinogens were widely used in tribal rituals, and the Incas used it in the form of peyote. A drink was concocted from the cocoa bean, and Indigenous people drank cassina, a caffeine-infused stimulant, across the east coast of America, the Gulf Coast all the way to the Rio Grande. If you are interested to know more about this little-known topic, a good place to start your education is with Elain Casy (1978) and her references. My point here is to challenge the myth advanced by some that substance use, let alone abuse, did not exist in the New World before the Europeans. This is simply not true. Since structure, what it means to be an addict, is cross-cultural, if there was use there is good reason to believe that abuse also existed. Why would it be otherwise?

The Europeans essentially were an alcohol-guzzling culture until they were introduced to opium and other exotic drugs from the Orient. I am reminded that the fictional Sherlock Holmes was a user of (addicted to?) cocaine, and similar period novels often refer to opium dens.

In the four quadrants of the world, some form of intoxicating substance has always been, and continues to be, used. Since there was use everywhere, experience supports a conclusion that along with it also came abuse everywhere, which means addicts were being created then as they are now. The prevalence of course, is unknown but it is probably reasonable to guess that it was at least proportional to population size. The magnitude of the problem then and now, I believe, equals its persistent, proportional existence. There is no benefit in pretending the problem did not exist among certain people in certain places. Substance use and abuse has been and continues to be a cross-cultural, global problem.

The tribal status quo is maintained, therefore, through a myriad of means, and one seems to be the creation of myths. While the exact purpose of this mostly escapes me, I am certain that the myth makers are benefitting from it. Also, for certain, a steady supply of addicts, who invariably become addicted and people who become addicted as a function of life circumstances, has grown into a huge business. Sadly, so far, we seem content to keep it that way. A terrible shame that we are because we can prevent this insidiously persistent, global problem. We can and we do - like Sally with her son, and like Robert's parents, who prevented him from becoming an addict. All that is required is the individual and collective will to do so. And, I reiterate, we have the rationale for what works, and why, when the problem exists and needs to be brought under control.

Tribes benefitting from the hardships of other tribes, as is evident over and over again, is a difficult arrangement to undo. Undoing this arrangement, therefore, must be one of the first tasks on our to do list.

INSIDIOUS BIOLOGY

By now, especially if you have read the previous three books in this trilogy, you know very well my disdain for applying the medical model where it does not belong. I have no issues with medicine when it is relevant to the problem, like an appendix that needs to come out. I have a huge issue, however, with talk of tribalism being hard-wired. The idea conjures up nerve networks and physical structures that are permanent and their effect on us not amenable to modification. This is a fatalistic, silly idea that most people unfortunately accept at face value. The idea's appeal is that it allows for the abdication of responsibility to do something about it.

Listening to the deniers of the COVID-19 pandemic and global warming, watching the persistent police and white supremacist violence perpetrated on people of colour, especially black, I am amazed that in the midst of all that absolutely no one talks of tribalism as the cause of it all. There is much talk of 'systemic' this and that and demands to stop it but no apparent awareness of the root cause. This is the price we all pay for the fatalistic idea that tribalism is hard-wired. To fix something we are told is in our physical make up, we might as well try to reverse where the sun rises and sets. No one even thinks of doing either.

With few seeming to be aware that the problem of tribalism is most people being cognitive developmentally stuck, and that this causes the madness that is the human condition, there is no one but you to draw attention to it. When you get comfortable with the idea, engage whomever you can, whenever you can, and create as much noise as you can, until people start to hear what they must.

IT'S ALL ABOUT PREVENTION

I have personally known hundreds of Sallys, who have predictably brought their addict propensities under control, however, not before suffering much and not before causing a great deal of suffering to those who care about them or depend on them.

Fortunately, with the benefits of the external source of heat provided through the Alcoholics (Addicts) Anonymous fellowship there is hope for those damaged during the early years. Would it not be better, however, to avoid, to in fact prevent, the damage from occurring in the first place? That is exactly what Sally decided to do with her son, just as so many abstinent addicts also have done and are doing.

The prevention part, experience has taught, is far easier and far more rewarding than the 'intervention' part. In the first book TWO, in this series, the story of Robert outlines what type of parenting and environmental conditions are necessary to achieve prevention by facilitating optimal development during the formative years.

The primary reason for telling Robert's story is to convey what can be done. What is being done over and over again all over the world, however, is tragically not enough.

For those of you who want to be proactive, who want to stop the intergenerational perpetuation of dysfunctionalities, especially the creation of an addict, I have one singularly important recommendation. Read a Manual. There are several outstanding authors who have written outstanding 'manuals' on parenting. My personal favourite, the one on my night stand, some thirty-five years ago, when my children were young is Barbara Coloroso's. "Kids are Worth It". I like her work because she provides an optimal, parenting policy from which doable actions flow. After her parenting policy book my second favourite book is Thomas Lickona's book "Raising Good Children". He makes you think about what kind of child you want to raise and then provides strategies for doing it.

While both books were published some years ago, they are as relevant now as they were when first released. Thankfully, both remain in print. There are of course other parenting books that deal with specific and generic parenting issues. The best criteria for selecting other parenting manuals is to look for ones that focus on facilitating the optimal activation of a child's developmental potential accomplished through empathic nurturance. Complex concepts, to be sure, but critically important to understand and implement if you want to be a competent parent.

ON BEING A DEVELOPMENTALIST

As a young clinician, like all new practitioners, I was consumed with the desire to be an effective therapist. I started out by emulating how famous clinicians conducted therapy sessions and immersed myself in their conceptual models. This phase, thankfully did not last long for several good reasons. The best reason being an emerging desire, and overwhelming need to do myself out of work. To accomplish this, I began to realise, requires the prevention of dysfunctionalities from occurring in the first place.

From this need to be an effective therapist, program design and implementer, and to prevent problems, to which I was responding, emerged my affinity to embrace the developmental model-perspective. Not only does the model serve well the requirement to explain a presenting problem, most often than not, a person behaving badly, it also serves well the task of knowing how to intervene. From a developmentalist perspective, the intervention is habilitative. The task is to promote the activation of a troubled person's cognitive developmental potential because how one thinks determines how one behaves. Tribal thinking leads to tribal behaviours, the best example of which, as described in this work, is racism in all its manifestations.

The added value, benefit of embracing the developmentalist perspective is that it so clearly reveals how to prevent a myriad of later-life negative consequences to early years adverse experiences. In the "Because We Can" book the third part is all about how to design and implement strategies for the effective activation of every child's innate, cognitive, developmental potential. Children whose potential is being realised, who do not get developmentally stuck, do not become adult clients. While it may take five generations to achieve this paradigm shift in the human conditions the developmentalist, psychosocial, perspective certainly makes it a doable and achievable undertaking.

The challenge is not so much in the doing as it is convincing establishment status-quo protectors of the need to do so.

WHAT IS YOUR CONCEPTUAL FRAMEWORK?

This is an incredibly important question that needs a great deal of elaboration to be answered well. By conceptual framework, I mean the glasses through which you see, understand, and explain the world you experience. From what consolidated ideas do you interpret the world and how people behave in it? Still not very clear, I know, so let me illustrate.

My conceptual framework, how I interpret, make sense of all that is good and bad about the behaviour of people in this world, is through the lens of a psychosocial cognitive developmentalist. Specifically, how environment impacts an individual's gift of cognitive developmental potentials. As in the first book, "TWO", when the environment is impoverished, the impact on the individual is catastrophically negative. Sally is made an addict, a person forever without a warm pot-bellied stove. In contrast, when the environment is infused with empathic nurturance, Robert is made to be a self-actualising "human becoming".

This is not a tribe-specific belief system. It is a conceptual framework based on a methodologically reliable and valid cross-culturally observed, invariant, hierarchical sequence of development. In other words, it's good stuff. What makes it an especially useful conceptual framework are two things: the first, is that it is cross-cultural. Development occurs the same way in the most isolated places on earth as it does here. Second, the conceptual framework has many doables embedded in it. There are things that can be done to facilitate development, and sadly, as we know by now all too well, to obstruct it. To answer the question as to your conceptual framework is to put into words a logical, coherent way of reasoning consistently applied to what you experience.

If your conceptual framework is that 'might makes right', you are at the first stage of cognitive development. If you see the world through the proverbial rose-coloured glasses, only see beauty and always use platitudes, or the exact opposite of this, you are at the second stage of reasoning, the hallmark of which is the creation of pleasing fantasies and the immediate satisfaction of needs.

If you explain the world's problems as caused by 'them' – immigrants, people of colour, recipients of social assistance, women in the workforce instead of in the kitchen, Muslims, Christians, Jews or the "one percent " – you are at the tribal reference group third stage of development. You are at the fourth stage of your developmental potential if your focus is on maintaining social order, doing what is expected of you and respecting the authority of those who have the knowledge and skills required by their role in society.

At stage five, your conceptual framework is focused on the greatest good for the greatest number. At this stage of reasoning, you can actually understand and live by the tenets of democracy and you respect the natural and legal rights of individuals. Your conceptual framework at the next stage is the super-social principled one discussed previously. Your focus is on treating everyone equally, regardless of who they are and regardless of the circumstances.

These brief examples define one set of several existing, conceptual frameworks. Given the theme of tribalism in this book, the harm created by it and the two stages coming before it, your task now is to locate your perspective. Next, you need to determine if you are satisfied with where you self-located the lens through which you interpret events and the behaviour of people. Does the lens serve you well? If the answer is "yes", and you located your conceptual framework at any of the first three perspectives, you are among the blissfully ignorant. If you are not satisfied with your conceptual framework and have not been for a long while, it's time to follow Sally's path and get busy. Leave your unfounded, tribal opinions and faith where they belong: in the dust bin. Get curious, reflect, read and learn to make formulations based on reliable, valid, observable, and measurable evidence. There is challenging but ultimately very rewarding work to be done. When you get tired, reflect on the fruits of Sally's efforts and that she is far from alone in activating the gift of developmental potential. Sally and many others are testaments to the work's doability. Life, indeed, is a continuous journey that is only done when it's done: when the lights go out for the last time.

Unlike the first three books, I am ending this fourth one with a series of challenges. Of course, it goes without saying, if you have a different perspective or even a better one than the theme of this book, speak out, start a debate, get people talking, and wait to see what comes from it.

Do not settle for endless talking-head descriptions of what you can see for yourself. Ask for explanations, for the very root cause of events and what people do. Then, ask for doable solutions based on the explanation.

Be constantly mindful of the difference between change and progress. At the very least, when you are settling for change, know that you are. But if you want progress, you have to know what it looks like. Take the time to know the important distinction. Practice and debate it, and when you are comfortable with your understanding of it, demand it. Do not settle for incomprehensible rhetorical platitudes when progress is required.

Be no longer satisfied with fatalistic, establishment-based, status-quo obstructionist strategies that claim complexity and a need for further analyses, study or investigation. Progressive explanations and solutions are simple. We have been, and continue to be, stuck at the tribal, cognitive developmental stage of reasoning and behaving. The challenge and complexity comes in the getting unstuck. The reason for optimism is because if the Sallys of this world can do it, we all can do it.

Be no longer satisfied with rage- and agenda-based destructive criticism of progressive ideas, no matter how loudly it is voiced. Demand to know what the critic's alternative explanation is and what actions based on it will bring about progress. If a key component of either the explanation or solution is 'faith', you are probably speaking to a religious, tribal person. If the key component of both involve observable and quantifiable variables, you are probably heading for progress. So, choose wisely.

I will end here with a wonderful interpretation of a Buddhist proverb:

> When the student (you) has
> surpassed the teacher (me),
> the teacher has succeeded.

REFERENCES

Armstrong, K. (2019). ***The lost art of scripture: Rescuing the sacred texts***. New York, NY: Alfred A. Knopf.

This text, exhaustively comprehensive, a challenge to read, both chronicles the intended purpose of written and oral scriptures, as well as the various iterations through which all religions evolved over the centuries. Initially, all started from an inclusive, tolerant perspective with a focus on the common good. A central theme is that scriptures were understood to be a significant means by which to learn, indeed gain the wisdom for which we all have the potential. Distortions ensued from the self-interest of individuals, from which always emerged various tribes almost always in conflict with each other. Worth the struggle to read.

Bettelheim, B. (1982). ***Freud and man's soul***. New York, NY: Vintage Books.

"The English translations of Freud's writings are seriously defective in important respects and have led to erroneous conclusions, not only about Freud the man but also about psychoanalysis." This, the first sentence in the book, says it all. I include this reference as a very clear example of how tribal agendas can rob us of value from which we could all benefit. It is a short, accessibly written book, well worth the time to read and see for yourself tribalism in one of its worst manifestations.

Buckingham, W., Burnham, D., King, P.J., Hill, C., Weeks, M., & Marenbon, J. (2011). **The philosophy book: Big ideas simply explained**. New York, NY: DK Publishing.

The subtitle of this wonderful, large book reveals why it is included as a reference in this series of books. It is not at all intimidating, even given the subject matter. The book, in fact, is enticing and very readable, as I hope these four books are. It will easily satisfy your curiosity about what people have had to say over the ages, and hopefully also fire you up to learn more about important ideas and who had them. The most important idea in the context of this book is the identification of our developmental stagnation.

Coloraso, Barbara (1994). **Kids are worth it**. Toronto: Summerville House Publishing.

First and foremost this is a policy book about parenting. To make her point, Coloroso presents three general types of parenting with which we are all familiar from observing or living them. Cleverly and forcefully her presentation leads the reader to conclude that only the one parenting policy produces results any parent, even inadequate ones, would want for a child.

An easy, absolutely makes sense read. Every child should come home from the hospital with this operational manual. As an added bonus it is never too late to apply the parenting policy tenets to any child, regardless of age or status.

Conrad, P., & Schneider, J.W. (1992). **Deviance and medicalization: From badness to sickness**. Philadelphia, PA: Temple University Press.

I include this reference as another excellent illustration of the influence tribal beliefs, values and ways of doing things have had on how we define human conditions, such as difficulty coping with life (mental illness) or abusing a virtually universally consumed beverage, alcohol (alcoholism). Definitions change essentially because tribal doctrine changes. Often empiricism, science, reason, and objectivity have very little to do with how we decide to think about the human condition, which is the central theme of this worthwhile book.

Dimond, J. (2005). **Collapse: How societies choose to fail or succeed**. New York, NY: Penguin Books.

The title explains why I reference this book. An otherwise well-written, researched, and organized work, because of the author's restricted perspective, it falls short of being the magnificent work for which it had the potential. The restricted perspective probably is tribal, probably, it is academic tribal. There is much descriptive prose and not very much explanation. There is even less effort at offering a solution to stop societies from collapsing. Nevertheless, the book was a bestseller - I believe, because it appeals to the obstructed developmental perspective of the majority, who are content to passively watch/observe without the curiosity to know the why of what is described.

Freedman, D.H. (2010). **Wrong: Why experts keep failing us - and how to know when not to trust them**. New York, NY: Little, Brown and Company.

This is a most excellent, informative read. I highly recommend it. I include it here as a source of elaboration about what a working hypothesis is at its best, as opposed to an agenda-driven tribal perspective disguised as science. It is also a cautionary source, lest people fool their tribal selves that they are not tribal, and lest they fool themselves that the evidence with which they support their contentions is flawless. Being real does not disempower, it just makes us work harder, is my takeaway from this book.

Johnson, H.R. (2016). **Firewater: How alcohol is killing my people (and yours)**. Regina, SK: University of Regina Press.

This accessibly written book from an Indigenous lawyer's perspective describes all that went horribly wrong between his people and the European imperialists. It is a story of subtle and outright genocide that continues to this day. While he offers a culture-based solution, "changing the story", the means to achieving it is challenging to discern.

Klein, E. (2020). **Why we're polarized**. Toronto, ON: Avid Reader Press.

A very thoughtful and well written book with actual strategies (solutions) for fixing a very broken American political system. It is full of examples of how political parties change without ever achieving the progress required to avoid the election of a president, such as the currently unelected one at the time of this writing. It is also interesting how he focused on a polarized nation with barely a reference to the myriad of tribal factions that perpetuate the obstruction of a nation's potential for achieving the greatness of which it brags yet remains far from being. An excellent read for political wonks.

Lickona, Thomas (1994). **Raising good children: From birth through the teenage years.** New York: Bantam Books.

Using valid and reliable empirical evidence, the author explains the cognitive, developmental perspective at each stage in a child's life. Based on the explanation he then provides habilitative strategies to ensure a child does not get stuck as so many unfortunately do and become markedly dysfunctional adults. To motivate and to maintain the resolve of parents to be optimally informed caregivers to their children, Lickona challenges the reader to be proactively deliberate in activating each and every child's innate, cognitive developmental potential. A very worthwhile effort to read, learn and most importantly apply the lessons provided.

Nolan, A. (1994). **Jesus before Christianity**. New York, NY: Orbis Books.

This book is not unlike Bettelheim's book about Freud. The same first sentence of the book could be repeated just exchanging Freud's name with that of Jesus and psychoanalysis with Christianity. It is another example of a great message distorted for tribal purposes. Instead of humanity benefitting from Jesus, who had many uplifting, liberating and developmentally conducive things to say, the distortions have oppressed and subjugated people. Instead of activating the gift of our developmental potential, the distorted message obstructs it. Not surprisingly, religious, tribal people who believe, value, and act on the distortions refuse to acknowledge the existence of this book, let alone read it.

Pinker, S. (2018). **Enlightenment now: The case for reason, science, humanism, and progress**. New York, NY: Viking.

First and foremost, this book provides all the reason you will ever need for optimism about progress. In excruciating, exhaustively researched detail, our ability to solve all kinds of problems is chronicled. The main ingredient for success is said to be the ability to reason. It is required to identify a problem and then solve it. While

Pinker identifies tribalism to be a problem, since it clearly persists, it is of no surprise that it is not described as a problem solved. Curiously, as a Harvard professor, he makes no mention of former Harvard developmentalist colleagues, such as Lawrence Kohlberg or Carol Gilligan or their contribution to offering a solution to getting unstuck from our tribalism.

Polgar, A.T. (2002). **Because we can we must: Achieving the human developmental potential in five generations.** Hamilton, ON: Sandriam Publications.

Once again, I shamelessly reference this geopolitical treatise that is as relevant now as it was when I wrote it. My purpose for including it here is to refer you to an elaborate example of what having a conceptual framework (that is not tribal) can get you. My other purpose is to refer you to an accessible description of our innate, cognitive developmental potential. Stage 6 in the cross-culturally observed, invariant, hierarchical sequence of development represents the ultimate expression of being social. Being a principled social person is light years removed from being tribal. Most importantly, I describe, explain and offer doable solutions.

OTHER REFERENCES TO TRIBALISM

Fortunately, I am not alone in identifying tribalism as a problem. A quick search will reveal that others have written about it mainly in the context of politics and, unfortunately, mainly in the context of it being a hard-wired way of being required to ensure survival. While I part company with most of the authors, I believe it is important to know their take on it, most importantly to discern if their perspective is tribal or not. To satisfy your cat-like curiosity, as a place to start, look for:

- Sarah Cavanagh
- Steven Hobfoll
- Jack Donovan
- Amy Chua
- Elizabeth Crouch Zelman

ACKNOWLEDGEMENTS

The usual suspects, once again, enabled the writing and production of this fourth book in the trilogy. Drina, my kindred spirit, understands and supports my commitment to bring about progress in the world. Her support graciously extends to putting our shared resources to where my ideas are. Hopefully, what we have done together will inspire others to do their part in getting unstuck from being tribal.

Once again, the intrepid Laura Riggs has delivered her services with exceptional skill, all in the midst of giving birth and tending to her brand-new progeny. Separately, but in synchrony with the scholarly David Angles, they edit, challenge ideas, words, and sentence structures to help me express in the best accessible language the theme of this book. They are both invaluable contributors to the process, aptly joined by Philip Austin, of Workhorse Design Studio, the genius behind the book cover designs of all my publications.

Last, but by no means least, there is the previously-described navigator of our group, Grant D. Fairley. In retrospect, he is and has been far more than that. Without his wisdom and skill gained from experience, both the quality and timeliness with which this and the previous three books came into print would have been far less. He completes the productive group that we have become.

ABOUT THE AUTHOR

'If ever tribal, it was for fleeting seconds', is the best way to characterise this seasoned, curious student of life. Never a self-promoter but a promoter of ideas with which to bring about progress, he has tilted at many windmills in his almost fifty-year, multidimensional career. By design and happenstance, he has gradually transitioned from advancing the lives of individuals, couples, families, and groups in the context of their environment to reaching out to all people through the written word. His singular purpose is to promote the activation of the developmental, potential gift everyone is born with.

www.ingramcontent.com/pod-product-compliance
Lightning Source LLC
Chambersburg PA
CBHW031451040426
42444CB00007B/1051